MW01001634

OUR FATHER SPEAKS

Volume 1

by C. Alan Ames

ISBN: 1-890137-40-5

*Complete segments, according to date, may be reproduced,
if done so in full, and proper credits are given.
Partial reproduction is not allowed without the express
permission of the author. No portion of this book may be
copied or reproduced out of context.*

© Carver Alan Ames — 1999

1st printing, October 1999 — 10,000 copies
Printed in the U.S.A.
by The 101 Foundation, Inc.

Books Available in the U.S. from:

The 101 Foundation, Inc.
P.O. Box 151
Asbury, NJ 08802-0151
Phone: 908-689 8792
Fax: 908-689 1957
www.101foundation.com
email: 101@101foundation.com

and also in the following countries:

New Zealand
Patrick J. Clegg
P. O. Box 31495
Lower Hutt
New Zealand
Phone & Fax: 644 566 5786

Ireland
Touch of Heaven
66 Landscape Park
Churchtown
Dublin 14, Ireland
Phone & Fax: 01-298 5403

England
Angelus Communications
22 Milbury Drive
Littleborough
Lancashire OL15 OBZ
England
Phone & Fax: 01706 372 674

Australia
Touch of Heaven
P. O. Box 85
Wembley
Western Australia 6014
Phone 089-275 6608
Fax: 61 89-382 4392

Australia—web: http://members.networx.net.au/~toheaven
Australia—email: toheaven@networx.net.au

This book is dedicated with love to
William and Doreen Bott,
And to the memory of my wife's dear brother,
Stuart Bott.

St. Mary's Cathedral

Address: Victoria Square, Perth, Western Australia, 6000
Telephone: (08) 9325 9557 Fax: (08) 9221 1716

FOREWORD

In writing this Foreword what can I say that has not already been testified to by theologians, priests and lay people throughout the world? All are of the common mind that in the presentation of his message, both spoken and written, Alan Ames is theologically and scripturally sound.

Our Lord says: "By their fruits shall you know them" (Matt. 7 [20]). By his personal behaviour; by the evidence of his inner calm and peace, and the constant refrain of God's love; by his obedience to the Pope, his Archbishop and Spiritual Director, and by his firm orthodoxy, Alan bears witness to the fruits of a spirituality firmly rooted in God the Father, in whose honour this book is written.

I recommend the book to the reader with confidence.

Fr. Gerard Dickinson .

Rev. Fr. Gerard Dickinson
August 13, 1999

INTRODUCTION

by Carver Alan Ames

Until the Father in His mercy came into my life, it was one full of sin and full of self. I still am overwhelmed by the depth of the Father's love that He should consider someone like me worthy of the opportunity of salvation through His Son and our Lord, Jesus Christ.

It is hard looking back, seeing all the wrongs I committed and to see how I hurt God by those wrongs. I think of my lack of faith that also must have hurt my Irish Catholic mother deeply. I think of the times I stole as a boy from the Church, not even thinking of it as the house of God.

I think of the people I hurt physically and emotionally as I lived a pride-filled and self-centered life. I think of the addictions I had that led me deeper and deeper into sin and despair. I think of how I treated my wife and children badly, so often ignoring their needs and only thinking of mine.

As I reflect on the past, and as the pain of that past wells up inside me, I also feel the gentle, peace-filled love of the Father touching me, and I feel His words soothing my very soul as He says, "I love you My son, and I am here for you, to help you to a better life in Me," and I feel secure in the knowledge this is the truth, not only for me but for all people.

I remember how the Father at first sent an angel to try and change me. I really did not listen to the angel, but our loving Father did not give up on me. Next, He sent St. Teresa of Avila who, with her very stern, direct, but loving manner, awoke me to the way I was living. Very soon a succession of saints began to instruct me on the way that the Father wanted me and all people to live.

The next three saints who came to me were St. Stephen, St. Andrew, and St. Matthew. They explained, along with St. Teresa, the importance of prayer, Holy Scripture, the Sacraments and obedience to God's commandments.

After some months, our blessed Mother Mary began to appear and talk to me. She explained how God had appointed her as every person's mother and that her role was to help people to come to know the completeness of God's love, which is the Father, and the Son, and the Holy Spirit.

Mother Mary told me that the Father wanted to give each of His children on earth many gifts, so that they could be happy in this life and find eternal joy with Him in Heaven in the next life. Blessed Mother showed me how the Father had created mankind equal and loved each person equally, and that if I loved the Father, I should try to love people in the same way.

Then, in the greatness of His love, the Father sent His Son Jesus to appear and speak to me. Immediately I fell in love with our Lord God, Jesus Christ, as each word He spoke seemed to open my soul to a new understanding of the truth of God. I found it hard to come to terms with the fact that the Lord God Jesus Christ loved me so much that He would come to me in this way, for I had committed so many sins and was probably one of the least worthy people for this to happen to.

The Lord touched me in a way that I had never before experienced...so gentle, so loving and so kind. He called me brother and He called me friend and I knew Him within me and I never ever wanted to lose this; I never wanted to be away from Him again, and I never wanted to hurt Him by sinning anymore.

The Lord Jesus Christ began to show me how far away from God I had been and what it had cost me in my life, but that no matter how bad I had been, if I sought forgiveness and did my best to change, God loved me so much He would forgive me and help me to live a good life in Him. The Holy Spirit came and, united with Jesus, filled me with joy in a way that I would have never thought possible.

Then, one day a warm, tender and loving voice spoke to me, saying, "I am your Father, call Me Papa." Now I felt the Father within me and around me. The Father welcomed me as family, and with hope and excitement, I embraced His welcome. The Father gave me many messages to guide and instruct me on how, if I wanted to love Him more, I should live.

Now I have a burning desire within to please God in all that I do. At times my heart feels as if it will burst with the love that now, by the grace of God, resides there. Often I am begging the Father, the Lord God Jesus Christ, and the Holy Spirit to help me open my heart more, so that I can love God in a deeper way. The feelings of love, peace, joy, happiness, hope, and security at times reach a crescendo, and God in His mercy lifts me into an ecstasy of His love.

The Father has told me repeatedly that His love is there equally for all people, and that being so, if others were to share in the words of help He gave to me and to try to live them as I am trying to, that many people would find a way of deepening their relationship with Him. So, with His encouragement, I collected many of the messages the Father gave to me and put them together in this book.

As you read the messages, you will see some scriptural references, while others have none. This is because in the beginning the Lord did not give me any references, but then in December 1995, the Lord began to do so.

When I am given a reference from Holy Scripture, it may be one or two lines, or only one or two words from a line. Sometimes two or three lines from different parts of Holy Scripture are combined to make the reference. The references at first were taken from either the Jerusalem or Douay-Rheims Bibles, but later, to avoid any confusion, my spiritual director (Fr. Gerard Dickinson, given to me in 1994 directly by Archbishop Barry J. Hickey, Archbishop of my diocese in Perth, Western Australia) and I, decided to use only the New American Bible for references.

I hope that those who read these words of the Father will find His love in every one. As I meditate on them, even though I have read them several times, I still feel a drawing towards the Father and often see the words in a completely different way than before. Whether it is one line, or a several-page message, the beauty, simplicity, and profundity of each one seems to jump from the page to touch my very soul.

I encourage whoever reads this book to first pray that the Holy Spirit will open up the mystery of the Father's words, so that they may be brought to a closer relationship with Him...one of Father and child.

I pray from the depth of my soul that those who share in what the Father has given me in this book will also share the experience of His wonderful, glorious, life-giving love in a way which will bring them to the knowledge that His love must be lived and shared with others...that by the power of His Holy Spirit, they will be given the gifts to do so.

Papa, Father, I thank You for loving me, a sinful man, and I pray You show me and many others how to love You more.

INTRODUCTION FROM THE FATHER

5/19/99

As people read My words, often they forget to meditate on the true meaning and just give a cursory glance at each word. How important it is that time is spent to think about what each sentence says and what it means in a person's life.

People should ask My Holy Spirit to lead them to a deeper understanding of the words I give to mankind, so that these words can come alive in their lives. My words are living words, but people can become dead to them by not putting into action what I say.

All that I give to mankind is given in love. Mankind needs to accept what I give in love and then to act in love on what I have given. So often they read, think they understand, and do little or nothing of what I have asked. This is no understanding at all!

Throughout the history of mankind I have given My guiding word to them, but frequently mankind has not listened and the results are there for all to see. Pain, suffering and sin abound in the world, where instead there should be love, peace, and hope. People need to listen to Me, their heavenly Father, and to follow the advice I give to them; if they do so, life will be good, for that is how I created it to be.

My words, My advice, and My help are there for all people, and for each person the message is the same. It is to love Me, your God, above all others and to love one another as I have loved you through My Son Jesus. It is a very clear directive, and yet to many it seems to be hidden behind a cloud of pride and of self. Sometimes this cloud obscures the message completely and all that can be seen is a haze of sin.

Once again I say to My children on earth, follow these words of love and live a good, a happy, and a fulfilled life.

Once again I say to My children on earth, I love you and I want you with Me forever.

Once again I say to My children, listen to your Father Who created you and Who knows what is best for you.

Listen My children, listen.

(*Sirach 42:18*—Their innermost being He understands. The Most High possesses all knowledge.)

<u>5/14/95</u>

Under the Cross stood not only the Mother of God
   but all mankind, for when My Son gave His life,
   it was placed His love over all of mankind.
Under the Cross wept not only the mother of God,
   but all of heaven, for when My Son suffered, all
   of heaven suffered with Him.
Under the Cross were not only the sins of this
   generation cleansed, but the sins of all
   generations.
Under the Cross now are few who willingly come to
   repent and come for forgiveness.
Under the Cross now all need to stand and share in
   Jesus' mercy.
Under the Cross now all need to seek the protection
   of Jesus' divine love.

<u>5/15/95</u>

Father of nations, Father of men, Father of fathers.
Creator of all, Creator of creation, Creator of love.
God of mercy, God of hope, God of eternal
   happiness.

<u>5/15/95</u>

Deep within each person, deep within their very
   soul, is the true being all were created to be.
Many ignore or hide away their true self, too
   frightened to let it free.
They are frightened because of the hurt, the pain,
   the lack of self-confidence, the lack of trust,
   insecurity, embarrassment, and so many other
   things that stop the true self shining through.
What most do not understand is that if they let
   their inner self shine, all else just fades away.
All the barriers, all the hurts, all just falls away to
   leave a pure spirit of love.

The strength that is needed to do this is there for
all. The strength is to be found through My Son
Jesus Christ, in communion with the Holy
Spirit.
Once mankind recognizes this and accepts it,
the child within will be set free to come to his
Father in heaven.

5/16/95

Most of mankind is seeking the truth; it is just that
most cannot see it, even though it is in front of
them.
Most of mankind is looking, but with eyes that
are closed.
If only they would open them and see, see the
truth, the only truth, the truth that is Jesus
Christ, Son of God.
Once they see, then they will know the true love
that is the truth.

5/19/95

My Son's life was a gift, a gift to mankind from Me,
and a gift from mankind to Me.
This is a divine mystery that none completely
understands, but many try to.

My friends look at this mystery and see the love.
My enemies look at this mystery and say how
foolish.

My children look at this mystery and find their
Father's hand.
My enemies look at this mystery and find nothing.

My followers look at this mystery and see the
beauty.
My enemies look at this mystery and see only
stupidity.

Those who belong to Me know the beautiful love
that was given by the Father's hand.
Those who deny Me look at this mystery and know
nothing in their foolishness and make reasons
for not believing.

5/20/95

Among My children are those who love as little
children, with a pure love.
Among My children are those who live as little
children, with a pure life.
Among My children are those who stay as little
children, always joyful.
These are the ones who show how life is to be lived,
these are the ones who show how to love, and
these are the ones all should try to be.

5/20/95

Children place many demands on their parents.
Parents in their love try to fulfil their children's
needs.
Sometimes however, it is better to leave a demand
unanswered to teach the children humility.
To grant all requests makes selfish children who
in the end hurt themselves and their parents.

5/24/95

Awaken the world to My love.
Awaken the world to My mercy.
Awaken the world to My forgiveness.
Awaken the world to My Son Jesus Christ Who is
loving mercy, and has given all so that mankind
can be forgiven.

5/25/95

Following the road to heaven, you meet many good
  souls who are walking the same path but on a
  different journey.
You will see many fall and stumble, some lying at
  the side of the road, unable to get up, some
  trapped by the snares along the way.
Be strong for them, help them up, set them free,
  and guide them home to Me.

You will find many obstacles trying to stop you
  helping; sometimes it is even those you try
  to help who want to stop you.
This is like the exhausted man who says, "Leave me
  here to die."
You know you cannot, even though he may resist.
You must help them all, you must not deny any,
  even your most dire opponent.
It is through helping My children that you find your
  own way home, so in fact they are helping you
  as well.

5/25/95

Tasting the love of Jesus is like tasting the sweetest
  wine; you want more.
Unlike wine, Jesus' love is never-ending so that the
  more you want, the more you get.

5/26/95

When you see others in distress, help them.
When you see others in need, give to them.
When you see others in pain, comfort them.
By doing this you reflect the love of God and by
  doing this you show how true Christians should
  live.

5/26/95

A petal falls from a flower and lands on the soil.
As the petal decays, it becomes food for the flower.
This is how the love you share becomes food for
    you, for it is returned to you by those you love.
As the petal mingles with the soil, so it nourishes
    that from which it came.
It is the same with love, as you share love and it
    mingles with the love of others, it is returned to
    you and nourishes your soul.

5/29/95

Success can bring joy and happiness, but it must
    also be remembered to be humble.
Success without humility is failure.
Success with humility is victory.

6/1/95

Following the path I lay out before you is hard
    unless you trust.
In trust, your steps are guided, your hand is held,
    and your heart is opened.
Trust, believe, and follow, and then walk to Me in
    love.

6/1/95

A man who trusts, loves, and hopes, is a man
    whose soul shines brightly.
A man who trusts in Jesus, loves for Jesus, and
    hopes because of Jesus, will have prayers
    answered.

6/1/95

If you see with eyes of love, life becomes a gift.
If you see with eyes of hate, life becomes a burden.

6/6/95

A son who loves his father is dear to his parents.
A son who loves his father is dear to the family,
And a son who loves his father is dear to those who
    know and love his father.

With your love of Me you are dear to Me.
With your love of Me you are dear to My family.
With your love of Me you become dear to My
    children on earth who love Me.

6/8/95

Love is so complete when you give yourself to it.
Love is so special when you receive it.
Love is so individual when you receive it in an
    unique way.
Love is Jesus, Jesus Who is completely in love with
    mankind in a special and individual way.

6/9/95

When you hold the love of God in your heart, you
    love everyone.
When you fill yourself with the love of Jesus, you
    want to help everyone.
When you open yourself to the Holy Spirit, you try
    to bring the Spirit to everyone.
To bring the Holy Spirit, show the love of God to
    everyone and bring the loving peace of Jesus
    to all.

<u>6/13/95</u>

All the gifts are there for the betterment of
  mankind.
All the gifts are there to bring My children to Me.
All the gifts are there for people to use to help My
  children better themselves spiritually and come
  home to heaven.

<u>6/14/95</u>

Faith of faiths, strength of strengths, love of loves...
  found in My Son Jesus.

Truth of truths, light of lights, grace of graces...
  found through My Son Jesus.

Hope of hopes, joy of joys, life of lives...
  found with My Son Jesus.

<u>6/15/95</u>

The way to find God is Jesus, for Jesus is God.
The way to find happiness is Jesus, for Jesus is
  happiness.
The way to find eternal life is Jesus, for Jesus is
  eternal life.
The only way is Jesus and all ways are Jesus.

<u>6/16/95</u>

A day of love is the best day to live.
A day of joy is the best day to have.
A day of truth is the best day to be.
This day should be every day, when you live with
  My Son Jesus, for He is the truth and the joy
  that comes from being in love, as Jesus is love.

6/16/95

Patience brings peace, and peace brings comfort.
Be patient with others, show the peace of God, and
bring comfort to those in need.

11/14/95

A way to true happiness is to pray.
A way to true happiness is to love.
A way to true happiness is to love to pray, and to
pray for love.

11/15/95

A light burns in your heart; let it shine on others.
A love grows within your soul; share it with others.
A fire blazes within your spirit; set fire to others.
The light of God creates the love you have and fills
you with the fire of the Spirit to share with your
family on earth.

11/16/95

When My Son lived and died for mankind, He
reaffirmed the commandments I had given.
When He gave His life He did not resist, even
though all the power of God is available to Him.
He did not kill or hurt those who abused, beat, and
finally crucified Him.
This reaffirmed My commandment: Thou Shalt Not
Kill.

What Jesus did was to show mankind that complete
trust in God was important, even unto death.
What Jesus did was show the importance of the
eternal life to come, and that this life is but a
stepping stone to that.

9.

The early Christians knew this, and this is why
they did not resist when they were beaten and
killed.
They trusted in God's promise of the next life and
were prepared to give all for it.

Today, people should understand that if they trust
in God completely, the rewards of heaven are
theirs.

11/16/95

In friendship, you bring My love to others.
In love, you become a friend of others.
In Jesus, become a friend and a love to all.

11/17/95

A disciple of Jesus must love always, even when
times are difficult.
A disciple of Jesus must become love, for Jesus is
love.
A disciple of Jesus must live for Jesus' love and
take that love to others.

11/18/95

A beautiful spirit resides within each body, waiting
to develop into the love it was created to be.
If you wipe away the stain of sin from anyone, you
will find their beautiful spirit underneath.
All spirits are beautiful from creation, it only
depends on how you live as to how they develop.

11/19/95

With the giving of His life, My Son Jesus showed
the greatest act of love.
He loved Me so much that with His dying breath, He
offered Himself to Me.
What complete love this showed, that through pain
and suffering He gave Himself to Me for
mankind.

How many people give up on God with the smallest
of problems?
These people should remember what My Son Jesus
endured and see how He still loved through it
all.
Then they should offer their pain to Me through My
Son Jesus and receive the graces that await
them.

11/19/95

When friends call, answer.
When friends call, be there.
When friends call, give.
All of mankind are your friends, so answer the call
and be there to give.

11/20/95

Find the peace that comes from being one with God,
by uniting with My Son Jesus in the Eucharist.

11/20/95

Listen to the Word and follow it.
Listen to your heart and follow it.
Listen to your Lord Jesus and follow Him.
Place the Word that is Jesus into your heart and
follow it.

<u>11/22/95</u>

When people offer their love to Me, it opens My
heart to fill them with My gifts.
When people accept My gifts, it fills My heart with
their love.
When people take My gifts to others it fills others
with My love, which is then returned to Me as a
gift.
What a divine mystery!

<u>11/23/95</u>

My Son comes only in love, and yet so many reject
Him.
My Son comes only to forgive, not to condemn, and
yet so many turn away from Him.
My Son comes only as a friend, and yet so many
fear Him.

It is strange how, when love, forgiveness, and
friendship are offered, they are spurned.
Yet, when hate, greed, and anger are offered, they
are welcomed.

<u>11/24/95</u>

Love, just love.
Trust, just trust.
Believe, just believe...
And all is possible.

<u>11/24/95</u>

Trusting your God for all your needs shows true
love.
Trusting your God for all your life shows true love.
Trusting your God to fulfill His promises in your life
as they are needed, shows you truly love God.

11/29/95

Into your heart put My love, and then surround
    your whole life with it, to find nothing can harm
    you.
You will only be frightened, worried, anxious if you
    do not trust in My love.
So trust, believe, love...and be at peace.

11/30/95

To understand another is difficult, so don't try; just
    love them.

11/30/95

Underneath the hard outer layers that many place
    in front of their true selves is a softness, a
    gentleness, a kindness that all have.
When you peel away the outer layers and set that
    beauty free, it is so sweet that every moment of
    life becomes a joy and everyone you meet
    becomes a friend.

12/1/95

Resting in My love brings peace,
Resting in My heart brings love,
Resting in My arms brings comfort.
Jesus...My love, My heart, and My ever-loving arms
    Who waits to embrace all My children in love.

12/3/95

Open your heart and show your love.
Open your heart and show the truth.
Open your heart and show how true is God's love.

13.

To give yourself to God, means to give yourself in
  love.
To give yourself to God, means to give to those in
  need.
To give yourself to God, means to give without fear
  of rejection.

This is the way of God.

12/6/95

The Lamb was slain, and a house was built.
The Lamb was slain, and evil was defeated.
The Lamb was slain, and heaven was opened.

12/6/95

Crossing a river can be easy if you use a bridge, but
  if you try to walk across the water, it can be
  difficult.
Jesus is the bridge to heaven.
If you walk with Jesus, then the way is easier.
If you walk by yourself, then you may be swept
  away by the flood of evil that covers the earth.

12/6/95

Peace, love, and hope.
Joy, happiness, and truth.
Jesus, Jesus, Jesus.

12/6/95

A fish swims with the current to make its swim
    easier.
A bird flies with the wind to gain greater altitude.
A flower reaches for the sky to bask in the sunlight.
The children of God must reach for the Son and be
    filled with His Spirit to make their climb to
    heaven easier.

12/7/95

Loving others brings joy,
Praising others bring happiness,
Sharing with others brings hope.

12/7/95

Sleep in love,
Sleep in joy,
Sleep in Jesus.

12/7/95

Immaculate, pure, and sweet.
Immaculate from conception.
Pure throughout life.
Sweet in her love of God...
Mary, My daughter.

15.

<u>12/10/95</u>

In each person I have placed My love.
It is there even in the most sinful person.
My love is within the heart and soul of everyone.
Often, though, it is denied; it is forced down and
   down so that it hardly shows.
There seems to be with many this constant struggle
   to ignore or deny My love, a struggle that
   accepts evil and denies good.

It is no wonder then, that so many people suffer
   from diseases, diseases of the spirit, of the
   body, and of the mind.
If you spend your life struggling, then the strain
   becomes too much, and it is because of this,
   that many problems occur.
The answer to many diseases begins with ending
   this struggle and letting My love naturally
   engulf you, lead you, and watch over you, as it
   is meant to do.

Why struggle against what is good for you?
If people would only accept My love and let Me fill
   their lives, then the beginning of a new healthy
   life spiritually, emotionally, and physically is
   theirs.

<u>12/11/95</u>

When you feel tired, take time to recover.
When you are feeling sore, take time to rest.
When you feel exhausted, take time to restore your
   energy.
If you do not, then you will only get worse, not
   better.

12/11/95

Remember the words of God,
Remember the love of God,
Remember to listen and to surround yourself with
    God's love.

12/12/95

A hand is offered to help, accept it.
A heart is offered to love, embrace it.
A mother offers her love with a hand that is always
    outstretched to guide and to embrace.

12/13/95

As I watch My children on earth, I look upon them
    with love, the love of their Father.
I want to share with them My love and bring them
    to dwell with Me in My house of eternal joy.
All it takes for this to happen is an acceptance of
    My love by My children.
Once they accept My love, then they will come to
    know what true life is.

12/13/95

Inside all of My children is a longing, a longing to
    be loved and to give love.
It is when this longing is denied, either by self or by
    others that, in the pain of denial, sin may
    flourish.
It may be the sin of hate, revenge, selfishness,
    greed and much more.
It is when this love is denied, that often pride rears
    its ugly head and leads the person deeper and
    deeper into sin, sin which is often justified by,
    "As no one cares for me, I will care for no one
    except myself."

17.

This justification is often hidden, reasons given to
    cover it up, but it is this that is the true reason.
If all were loved and could express their love, then
    the pain of feeling unwanted, unloved would
    disappear.

What My children should see is that no matter who
    they are or what they do, I love them and I want
    their love.
If they accept My love and give Me their love, they
    will find that the pain disappears and only joy
    will fill their hearts.

12/14/95

Looking upon the sadness of those who mourn, see
    My love as a way of bringing peace and comfort.
See My love as their rock to lean on.

12/14/95

Forgiveness comes with love,
Frustration comes with self.

12/14/95

A prayer can be so much; it can be an expression of
    love, of faith, of hope.
A prayer can be so little; it can be an
    inconvenience, a duty, a chore.

A prayer can be answered when it is filled with love,
    with faith, with hope...for it is then that you
    truly accept God's will.

12/14/95

Underneath the outer layers that cover most of My
children's hearts is a beautiful flower of love.
When these flowers are exposed and unite in My
love, they give the sweetest perfume...the
fragrance of love.

12/16/95

A friend who helps from his heart, is a true friend.
A friend who wants the best for you, is a true
friend.
A friend who understands your feelings and
considers them, is a true friend.
Become a friend to all, and in My name, open their
hearts.

12/16/95

The two hearts of Jesus and Mary become one.
The two loves of Jesus and Mary become one.
The two hopes of Jesus and Mary become one.
One in Jesus, to bring the love of God to all.

12/17/95

To pray in friendship shows true love.
To pray with a friend shows true love.
To pray in public shows true love.
When you join with a friend to pray in public, you
show your love of Me and your true friendship
with your brothers and sisters.

19.

12/18/95

Be truthful, always.
Be open, always.
Be Mine, always.

12/18/95

Inside your heart, find My love,
Inside your heart, find My peace,
Inside your heart, find My love and peace to give to
    others.

12/25/95

A season of joy,
A season of happiness,
A season of love,
My Son's birthday.
How many do not know the wonder of this time?
How many are unhappy?
How many do not know love?
Take My love with joy and happiness to all, so that
    they, too, may know the wonder of God's love.

21/21/95

The help a willing heart gives, is a special treasure.
The support a converted soul gives, is a special
    grace.
The strength a changed spirit gives, is a special gift.
Help others and support them in times of need.
Become their strength to change their hearts and
    give their souls to God.

12/21/95

Love means loving all,
Love means forgiving all,
Love means no conditions.

12/21/95

In front of all mankind is the offer of peace, joy,
    and happiness.
It is an offer I will always make, an offer of love.

12/21/95

From among the people, there have always arisen
    great prophets, great saints, and great servants
    of God.
What this shows mankind is that I choose anyone,
    no matter his standing, his position.
I choose those I know will follow My will completely.
It also shows that anyone who opens his heart to
    Me can become a true servant of Mine.

12/29/95

Placing all of your hopes and aspirations into My
    Son's hands will bring them to fulfillment.
When you ask in love, your prayers will be
    answered, and when you ask in humility, your
    life will be fulfilled.

21.

A book of names is held in heaven.
In the book are all those who belong to Me.
In this book are the names of God's chosen and
    those who in return chose God.

Each time I look upon this book, My heart is filled
    with joy, the joy a Father has when He knows
    His children love Him.

12/29/95

In the beginning, I was.
Always, I am,
And forever, I will be.
A mystery mankind can never understand, a
    mystery that should be accepted in faith.
So many, though, because they cannot understand,
    refuse to believe.
So many refuse to see.
So many refuse to trust.
All came from My love; this is the truth, but how
    many believe?
All is created by My love, but how many accept
    this?
All is formed from My will, but how many see this?
I am the beginning.
I am always,
And I am throughout eternity.

12/29/95

As you feel the wind gently blowing on your face, so
    feel My love touch your soul.
As you feel the tenderness of a loved one's embrace,
    so feel My love caressing your soul.
As you feel the joy of being in love, so feel My love
    fill your soul.

1/2/96

To trust is important, for it is in trust that all is
    possible.
To believe is important, for it is with true belief, you
    can give all for God.
To trust what you believe is true, is the most
    important aspect of your love for God, for
    without it what love is that?

1/2/96

What you feel is human...your fears, your doubts,
    your wondering.
To be human is to feel this way, and to be God's is
    to overcome these feelings.

1/7/96

A son of Mine loves all.
A son of Mine serves all.
A son of Mine helps all.
It is in your help of others that you show your
    service to Me, and you show others your love of
    God.

(Ephesians 2:10—For we are His workmanship,
    created in Christ Jesus in good works, which
    God has prepared that we should walk in them.)

1/10/96

To share in love means to trust those with whom
    you share.
You share in My love, so trust in Me.

23.

1/11/96

The peace of God reigns supreme in the hearts of
those who follow Jesus.
Sometimes this peace is disturbed by the turmoil of
evil and the humanity of the person.
In these times, if the person looks to Jesus in
prayer and the sacraments, God's peace will
return, and with it, the love of God as a barrier
against evil.

1/11/96

To look upon My Son hanging in pain on the cross,
filled My heart with sorrow.
To see how My Son, Who only brought love and
forgiveness, could be treated so, brought tears
from My heart.
To see God's Son abused, rejected, beaten, and
killed, confirmed how much mankind needed to
be forgiven and why his redemption was
necessary.

(Matthew 20:32—Lord have pity on us, Son of
David.)

1/11/96

In moments of doubt, think of Jesus on the Cross,
and see that it was mankind's doubts that put
Him there.
In moments of temptation, think of Jesus on the
Cross, and see that it was mankind's weakness
that put Him there.
In moments of love, think of Jesus on the Cross,
and see that it was God's love of mankind that
put Him there.

(Luke 23:34—Father forgive them, they know not
what they are doing.)

1/11/96

To spend a day with your Father, brings joy to My
  heart.
To show your love of your Father, brings happiness
  to My spirit.
To show your obedience of your Father, brings
  peace to your heart and fills you with My Spirit.

1/15/96

To discern can be a difficult task, but go with your
  heart.
Uneasiness, pain, and discomfort do not come from
  God...only peace and tranquility.

1/16/96

When you express your love for Me, feel the joy in
  your heart.
This is there for all people, if they, too, would show
  their love.

1/16/96

Love given is love magnified.

1/16/96

As love grows in your heart, so it grows around you
  as you bring your love to those you meet.

1/16/96

There is a path that leads to heaven; it is the path
of Jesus.
There are many paths that lead from heaven; they
are the paths of evil.
Sometimes it is hard to see which path is the right
one, as so many tricks and lies are used to
deceive and lead people from the true path.
If, in humility and love, you walk along the road of
life and see yourself for what you are, a child of
God, and recognize the truth in the Word Which
is Jesus, then you will make it home to heaven.

1/18/96

In the light of My love, only good can live.
In the light of My love, only truth can be.
In the light of My love, only joy can be found.

(*John 12:36*—Believe in the light.)

1/18/96

The joy of love,
The peace of love,
The hope of love.
Jesus, Who is love.

Love, complete love.
Love, glorious love.
Love, true love.
Jesus, Who is love.

The Lord of love,
The Lord Who is love,
The Lord Who is God...
Jesus.

1/19/96

A bird flies freely and trusts in God. Become as the
bird.

1/19/96

I am, I was, I will be,
Now, forever, always...
God.

1/20/96

In faith, all is possible.
With trust, all can be.

In love, faith becomes strong.
In humility, love is true.

In commitment, all is given.
In service, all is received.

1/20/96

When you do My work, believe.
When you do My work, have faith.
When you do My work, be humble.
When you do My work, show love.
When you do My work, you show your commitment
and your service to Me.

1/20/96

What a joy when you do My work.
A joy for Me to watch, and a joy for you to give.

27.

1/20/96

Have faith, and see the love of God touch those in
    need.

1/20/96

My work is there...do it.
My love is there...share it.
My heart is open...ask.

1/21/96

The joy of saving souls,
The love of bringing hope,
The mercy of God.

1/21/96

Humility, love, and truth...all from God, all for you.

1/22/96

My friends are your friends,
My family is your family,
My church is your church.
Bring all to My friendship through My church, and
    make them part of My family.

1/22/96

They came in search of God, and I filled them.
Now that they have found Me it is important they
    continue to search, and do not think there is no
    more.

1/22/96

See in children the pure love all should have.
See in children the complete trust all should have.
See in children the hope for the future all should
    have.

1/23/96

Prayers from the heart are received into My heart.
When you struggle with prayers, if they are from
    the heart they are good prayers, so do not feel
    they are not worthy.

1/25/96

Every moment a prayer,
Every thought a gift,
Every action a glorification of God.
See your life this way, and let all see My love in
    you.

1/25/96

Within each person see My love, and bring it forth
    with prayer and in hope.
Within each person see what can be, and pray for
    them.
Within each person see a brother or sister you love,
    and open your heart in prayer for them.
It is in this way you help them become their true
    selves in Me.

1/25/96

The prayers open hearts; the Spirit fills hearts, and
    the hearts become God's.

1/25/96

As the rays from the sun supply the light and the
    warmth that is needed for life, let the rays of My
    Son Jesus light up your soul and warm your
    heart.

1/25/96

On a throne of gold, I sit in glory...the glory that is
    God.
On a throne of gold, I sit in joy...the joy that is love.
On a throne of gold, I sit and wait for My children
    to share in My love that will fill them with joy
    and bring them to My glory.

1/25/96

It is within each person to be good or to be bad, to
    sin or not to sin.
Each person has a free choice, and it is by these
    choices that they either grow or diminish.
Every day, every moment is a choice, a choice to
    say yes to good or yes to evil; there is no
    in-between.
With so many choices to make, it is no wonder that
    many sometimes make the wrong ones, and it is
    no wonder so many are confused.

If each person was to become as a child who puts
    complete trust in his parents to guide him
    safely through life until he is mature enough to
    make his own decisions,
If each person could accept Me as their parent and
    let Me guide them through the choices they
    have to make, then they would find that the
    choices they make are the choices for good, that
    lead them to a peaceful, joyful, and eternal life.

1/28/96

It is so easy to fall into the trap of the evil one.
Stop it with prayer, before it leads you into despair.

1/28/96

Look at a flower and see its beauty; where does it
    come from?
How does it grow to be so glorious?

Look at the animals and see their joy in life, their
    complete trust in God.
How did they get this?

Look at the people and see their individuality, their
    differences and yet their sameness.
How could this be?

The beauty of life is a gift that, when it is allowed to
    grow freely in My love, becomes a joy.
With trust in God that everything will be supplied
    for its existence, life becomes a glorious
    treasure to be enjoyed.
With this trust, comes love of each other,
    acceptance of each other's differences, and
    seeing each person as part of the same family,
    the family of God.

1/31/96

Trusting brings strength, strength in My love.
Trusting brings hope, hope in My love.
Trusting brings joy, joy in My love.

Trust that My love answers your hopes and will fill
    you with joy.

1/31/96

In trust, in hope, in faith, in love, in God, all is
  possible.

2/4/96

To offer help to others is what you must do at all
  times.
In the offering, you must show love, and in the
  accepting, they should show respect for your
  wishes and your needs, also.

2/5/96

It is in your heart,
It is in your soul,
It is in your very being...
What is?
My love, for it is from My love that you were
  created.
When you understand this truly, and see that you
  are created as love, that is when you will
  achieve your destiny in Me.

2/6/96

The start of a day, the beginning of a wonderful gift,
  the dawn of eternity.
Each day is a wonderful gift I give to mankind.
Each day can be the start of the walk to Me, and
  can lead to eternal love.

2/6/96

The heart of men can be strong in Me or strong in
    self.
The first leads to joy, the second leads to nowhere,
    except sorrow.

(*Proverbs 7:1*—My Son, keep My words and treasure
    My principles; keep My principles and you will
    live.)

2/7/96

The Holy One, My Son Jesus, always hears you and
    brings your prayers to Me in love.

2/7/96

The time you spend with Me is the time you grow.
You may not see this or understand it; you may feel
    that you are struggling or that you are failing,
    but see that you do grow, for recognizing these
    feelings is part of it.

2/8/96

The Rosary, full of love, full of life, full of
    forgiveness, full of God.

(*Isaiah 8:3*—I went to the prophetess; she conceived
    and gave birth to a Son.)

33.

2/8/96

The prayer of love in union with your mother.
The prayer of the life of My Son Jesus.
The prayer of the forgiving love that brings life in
    God to those who open their hearts and see the
    truth of this beautiful prayer.
The prayer that is the Rosary.

2/8/96

Another question arises in your heart, another
    wondering what will be, another looking to the
    future.
Just trust...trust in God...trust in Me.

(Isaiah 50:10—Let him trust in the name of
    Yahweh; let him lean on his God.)

2/8/96

Trust brings strength, the strength of love.

2/11/96

If you were to look down a well, you might not see
    the bottom but you would know that it was
    there.
It is the same with My love; you may not be able to
    see it, but know that it is there.

2/11/96

Wrap yourself in My love; then bring others into its
warmth and peace as well.
Love shared is true love; love saved for oneself is an
insecure love.
Share My love and spread My security to all your
family.

2/12/96

In the heat of the day, rest.
In the heat of My love, be at peace.
In the heat of the moment, be calm.
In the heat of battle, be strong.
In the heat of anger, forgive.
In the heat of trials, overcome.
In the heat of rejection, love.

(*Matthew 11:29*—Shoulder My yoke and learn from
Me, for I am gentle and humble in heart, and
you will find rest for your souls.)

2/15/96

In your heart find love.
In your heart find peace.
In your heart find Me.

In your soul see God's love.
In your soul see God's peace.
In your soul see Me.

In your spirit place My love.
In your spirit place My peace.
In your spirit place Mine.

Your heart and soul, when filled with My Spirit, will
set many hearts on fire, the fire of God.

2/18/96

It takes love to understand the feelings of others
and love to answer their needs...be that love.

2/20/96

Success means not how much money you make but
how many souls you save.

2/23/96

A Man one day came before Me and asked for the
forgiveness of mankind.
He offered in atonement His Body and Blood,
He offered Himself.

This Man showed all mankind that to sacrifice
yourself for others is the greatest act of love you
can offer your brothers and sisters.

Yes, this Man was and is God, is Jesus.
Jesus showed that in love no sacrifice is too great.

This message is often ignored and rejected, but it is
the message of truth.
Mankind needs now to sacrifice for each other,
sacrifice in love, sacrifice in giving, and
sacrifice in hope.
Then the true love mankind has hidden away will
shine brightly, and peace will return to earth.

2/25/96

In peace find love, for where there is love there is
    peace.
In hope find love, for where there is love there is
    hope.
In truth find love, for where there is love there is
    truth.
My Son Jesus is the peace, the truth, the hope to
    be found in love, for He is love.

(*Esther 3:13/7*—Henceforth enjoy perpetual
    stability and peace.)

2/25/96

To leave your cares behind, look to My love.
To leave your worries where they belong, look to My
    heart.
To leave your fears in the distance, look to My gifts.

In the sacraments find My love.
In the sacraments enter My heart.
And in the sacraments find My gifts.

(*John 14:1*—Do not let your hearts be troubled;
    trust in God.)

2/25/96

To be with your Father in heaven, follow Jesus.
Jesus, My Son, will lead you by the heart and bring
    you to Me.

37.

2/25/96

To see the beauty of creation in all things, is a gift.
To see My hand in all that exists, is a grace.
To see the union of love throughout creation, the
    union of God, is a gift that gracefully leads you
    to understand My love.

2/26/96

My Son Jesus came to forgive sinners, came to lead
    the lost home, and came to show God's love.
When you imitate My Son, you must do the same:
    forgive, lead, and love.
When you do this, then the light of Jesus can be
    seen in you.

2/26/96

A man who works for God also works for his fellow
    men, for when you do God's work, it means
    helping and loving others.
Sometimes people profess to love Me and do My
    work, but they treat their fellow man with no
    love, just closed hearts.
How then can they do My work or love Me truly, if
    they do not love and help as I ask?

(Deuteronomy 5:32—This is what Yahweh our God
    has commanded.)

2/26/96

Into your heart place your brothers and sisters.
When you do this, you open your heart to Me.

2/28/96

Find peace in My heart,
Find love in My heart,
Find hope in My heart.
My heart, open to you through My Son Jesus.

2/29/96

My people are lost.
My people are confused.
My people are misled.
Through My Son, Jesus, they can be found, the
    confusion cleared, and the path become
    obvious.

(*Ezekiel 18:31*—Shake off all the sins you have
    committed against Me, and make yourself a new
    heart and a new spirit.)

3/1/96

Praise the Lord Jesus for His strength given to you
    through the sacraments.
Praise the Holy Spirit for His gifts given to you
    through the sacraments.
Praise the Father for His love given to you through
    His Son, Jesus, and magnified through the gifts
    of the Holy Spirit.

3/1/96

When you feel tired, rest.
When you feel lost, pray.
When you feel empty, receive the sacraments.
The tiredness, emptiness, and feeling lost are all
    signs that you are in need of My strength, found
    through prayer and the sacraments.

39.

3/6/96

Your prayers become a chain of love in the Rosary.
Your prayers become a bouquet of flowers in the
Rosary.
Your prayers become joined with My daughter,
Mary's prayers to make a beautiful love song
offered to Me.

3/6/96

Never rush, take your time.
Never fear, be calm.
Never worry, trust.

3/7/96

A man one day looked upon a woman and said, "I
am your master, you are inferior to me!"
From this moment, men came to believe this.

Through time women have been treated as inferior,
as less than men.
What pride, what arrogance to do this!

I created woman and I created her equal with man
to be his partner in life.

How then can men treat women differently from
themselves?
This is a sin, the sin of pride and the sin of denying
My creation its true place on earth, and that is
alongside man, not beneath him.

3/7/96

In the Church there are many different roles, some
    for men and some for women.
I appointed some men to be My priests and some
    women to help in their service as nuns.
Two different roles, but both so important.

If all look in humility to what I ask, then the
    Church will be strong, but if some look with
    pride and self, the church will be weak.

Today, in many, pride is to the front, and thoughts
    of how they can better themselves or fill the
    roles that were not meant for them.
If this path is followed, the Church is weakened.
If this path is denied, the Church will be
    strengthened.

Look within your hearts, My religious, and see if
    you follow Me or your pride.

(*Proverbs 14:8*—To the man of discretion, wisdom
    means a watch on his own conduct, but the
    folly of fools is delusion.)

3/7/96

My love is all around you,
My love is waiting to fill you,
My love is there for you.

3/7/96

The Father gives because He loves.
The Son offers Himself because He loves.
The Spirit touches because He loves.
One love, one God, one truth.

3/7/96

A fountain of love flowed from My Son's side on the
Cross.
It flows over the world and around all people,
washing them clean and filling them with love
when they accept this gift in humility.

(Daniel 7:14—On him was conferred sovereignty,
glory, and kingship, and men of all peoples,
nations, and languages became his servants.)

3/8/96

In prayer, you find before you the life of Jesus.
In prayer, you feel the love of Jesus.
In prayer, you see the glory of God in Jesus.

Prayer, a wonderful gift.
Prayer, a special grace.
Prayer, a glorious sign of love.

(Mark 11:24—I tell you therefore, everything you
ask and pray for, believe you have it already
and it will be yours.)

3/11/96

The joy you find in prayer is a grace I offer you.
The love you share in prayer is a gift I offer you.
The life you discover in prayer is a life for God, by
God's grace and as a gift of God, a gift which is
offered to all which, by My grace, will bring
them to life in Me.

3/11/96

To want to help is admirable.
To offer help, true love.
To give help, a prayer.

3/12/96

Today open your spirit in prayer, prayer from the
heart.
Today open your heart in prayer, prayer that fills
you with My spirit.
Today pray, pray, pray!

3/13/96

My love surrounds everyone the same, but most do
not recognize it.
They exist by My love, but most do not understand
this.
My love is in everything and everywhere, though not
many believe this.
If they did, the planet, the animals, and fellow man
would not be treated as they are.

3/13/96

A just man shares with all.
A just man forgives all.
A just man loves all...
My Son, the Just One, shares His love with all and
offers forgiveness to all.

(*Ecclesiasticus 11:17*—The Lord's gift remains
constant.)

43.

3/13/96

For too long mankind has lived in sin.
Now is the time to change, now is the time to love,
  not hate...
Now!

3/14/96

Each day, see My love before you.
Each moment, feel My love in you.
Each step, feel My love guiding you.
My love, Jesus.

3/17/96

In praise of God, spend your life.
In thanks to God, spend your life.
In love of God, spend eternal life.

3/17/96

A saint is what all are created to be, but it is up to
  the individual to accept this or deny it.
Some accept it completely in life and become saints
  on earth, while others struggle and take a little
  longer to achieve sainthood.

(Psalms 116:18—I will walk in Yahweh's presence in
  the land of the living.)

3/18/96

Making your life a gift to Me makes your life
  complete.

3/18/96

A friend who helps without seeking reward, is a
    true friend.
A friend who helps because of love, is a stout
    friend.
A friend who helps for God's glory, will be a friend
    throughout eternity.

3/20/96

In thanks, pray.
In love, pray.
In Me, pray.

3/20/96

A house of love,
A house of hope,
A house of God,
A house that prays.

3/20/96

It is good to think of Me in those moments of time
    with nothing to do, for then those moments
    become moments of love which are valuable to
    your heart and soul.

3/20/96

In your life, see My love.
In your life, live My love.
In your life, share My love.
Then you become a light in the dark to lead others
    to Me.

45.

3/20/96

My Son, Jesus, offers His heart each moment to
    mankind.
My Son, Jesus, offers His sacrifice each moment to
    mankind.
My Son, Jesus, offers His forgiveness each moment
    to mankind.

Each moment, a moment of love.
Each moment, a moment of forgiveness.
Each moment, a moment of mercy.
Take each moment and accept it for what it is...a
    gift from Jesus to you.

3/21/96

When you do My work, you are filled with love.
When you do My work, you share My love.
When you do My work, you become love.

3/21/96

The strength you need is found in the sacraments
    and prayer.
Remember this always.

3/22/96

Hanging on the cross was the love of God: rejected,
    abused, scorned, and crucified...but even then,
    the love remained.
The love that is offered to all.
The love that is God's forgiveness.
The love that can never die.
The love that is.

(*Jeremiah 51:17*—At this all men stand stupefied,
    uncomprehending.)

3/24/96

If you follow My Son, you reach heaven.
If you follow My Son, you bring Me joy.
If you follow My Son, you become part of My family.

In heaven you will find the greatest joy of all, as
part of My family.

3/24/96

A son may often ignore his parents, but when it is
important, he seeks and listens to them.
This is a sign of trust and love.
It is just that it is difficult at times for some to
show it.

3/24/96

My Son, Jesus, is always by your side to love, to
guard, and to guide.
My Son, Jesus, is always by your side to
strengthen, to encourage, and to help you
decide.
My Son, Jesus, is always by your side to watch, to
help, and to make evil run and hide.

(*Psalms 107:1*—Give thanks to Yahweh, for He is
good; His love is everlasting.)

3/24/96

My daughter, Mary...complete giving, complete love,
complete in God.
My daughter, Mary...love of God, love of man, love
of all.
My daughter, Mary...mother of God, mother of man,
mother of mercy.

47.

3/24/96

Two hearts of love: Jesus and Mary.
Two hearts of giving: Jesus and Mary.
Two hearts of peace: Jesus and Mary.

(*Zephaniah 3:14*—Shout for joy, daughter of Zion.)
(*Corinthians 13:11*—Be united: live in peace, and
the God of love and peace will be with you.)

3/27/96

Working for Me brings the greatest reward of all, My
love in heaven.

3/27/96

In love, accept the gifts of the sacraments, and then
in love, share your gifts.

3/31/96

A Father's love, a love for all His family.
A Father's hope, a hope for all His children.
A Father's care, a care to help all of His children
and hope for their future.

3/31/96

In your heart, find humility.
In your heart, find love.
In your heart, find Me.

3/31/96

Love Jesus, love the Spirit, love Me, your Father,
and find the Trinity of love filling you.

3/31/96

The fruits of the Spirit are there for all to see.
The gifts of the Spirit are there for all to have.
The servant of the Holy Spirit is there in humility.

(*Psalms 78:7*—So that they, too, would put their
confidence in God, never forgetting God's
achievements.)

3/31/96

Love shared becomes love strengthened.
Love given becomes love enriched.
Love offered becomes love living.

(*Song of Songs 2:2*—As a lily among the thistles, so
is my love.)

3/31/96

If you think of the need of others, you think with
your heart open.
If you think of your own needs, you think with your
mind closed.
If you open your mind to others, it becomes one
with your heart and one with Me.

4/1/96

Your mother Mary is with you every moment of your
life...watching, caring, helping, loving, and
guiding you deeper into My heart.
Take Mary's hand and find the way to Jesus, the
Holy Spirit, and Me, your Father.

49.

4/3/96

To share completely,
To give completely,
To love completely...is to do My will.

4/5/96 (Good Friday)

Every moment of this day...a moment of sadness,
    a moment of pain.
Every second of this day...a second of anguish,
    a second of abuse.
Every moment My Son Jesus lived on this day,
    was a moment of sadness to Him and a moment
    of great pain of body and soul.

Each second that passed was filled with anguish as
    My Son Jesus was abused and killed.

My Son Jesus, pure and sweet, full with pain and
    suffering.
My Son Jesus, awakening the world to God and
    answering the need in the world, the need of
    forgiveness.

4/5/96

How strange it must seem to many that God in His
    Son Jesus would accept such a death as
    crucifixion, the death of a sinner.

If mankind could see the passion of My Son Jesus
    for what it truly is, and then accept what is
    offered, sin would disappear from their hearts.

What Jesus did on this day was to carry all of
    mankind's sins in His heart and then pay the
    price for them.
In this way, Jesus paid for the sins of each person.

He took their suffering as His own, and then in
complete and humble love, cast them back to
where they belong.

Jesus stood in place of each person, and for that
person overcame sin.
It is only up to the person to accept this to receive
the forgiveness that is offered.

With the denial of this gift, many turn their backs
on the greatest gift ever offered by God: the gift
of redemption...and with this rejection, open
the doors to eternal damnation, where they will
have to pay the price themselves for their sins.

(*Psalms 106:8*—For the sake of His name, He saved
them to demonstrate His power.)

4/5/96

As My Son Jesus suffered, so did I.
As My Son Jesus gave, so did I.
As My Son Jesus offers, so do I.

Jesus, One with Me, unified with My Spirit, and
together united as the One True God.

4/5/96

Walking with Jesus means sharing with Jesus,
sharing in His love, His pain, and His
forgiveness.

4/5/96

My Son suffers each time a sin is committed.
Each sin a thorn in His crown, and each sin a nail
in His body.

4/6/96

The hope that is awaiting mankind lies sleeping.
The joy that is awaiting mankind lies resting.
The truth that is awaiting mankind lies peacefully
    in My arms.

Jesus, the Hope, the Joy, and the Truth that will
    arise and free mankind.

4/11/96

My Son on the cross, Myself on the cross.
My Son on the cross, mankind on the cross.
My Son on the cross unites mankind with God
    through His love.

(*Isaiah 22:24*—On it they will hang the glory of his
    Father's house.)

4/15/96

Stepping out in love, for love brings peace to those
    who listen.
Stepping out in hope, for hope brings joy to those
    who hear.
Stepping out for God brings hope to those who
    listen and fills them with My love, which brings
    true peace.

Step out and take My love wherever it is needed.
Step out and take My peace wherever there is
    turmoil.
Step out and take My hope wherever there are
    people.
Step out for Me and show the world you love Me.

4/18/96

It is right to trust, but within that trust you have
the responsibility of walking the right path;
otherwise you stop or delay what should
happen.

4/18/96

When together, be as one.
When apart, stay the same.
When united, be as one in Me.
Together you are one, apart you are one, in
marriage, one in Me.

4/20/96

In My hands I have enough for all, but who believes
it?
In My heart I have love for all, but who wants it?
In My Son I have forgiven all, but who understands
it?
I offer all and ask for little in return...all I ask for
is love.

4/22/96

A man was fishing one day, and as he sat quietly
staring into the water, he started to think about
the fish in the water and what a wonderful
creation they were.
He thought about how the water was there for them
and how all they needed to survive was in the
water.
What an incredible bond between the fish, the
water, and the food the fish ate.
All there in harmony, all there without worrying
about why, just accepting that it will continue
to exist and continue to be there forever.

53.

He wondered why mankind wasn't so trusting in
   creation; he came to see everything was here for
   man, just as it was for the fish.
Everything had always been here; it was only that
   he hadn't recognized this before.
He then started to think how wonderful is creation,
   the way it is designed to supply all that is
   needed; everything in creation working in unity
   to renew and continue what has been given.

Then he thought, with such a complex system
   throughout creation, it is impossible that it is
   chance that caused this to happen, for there
   seemed to be a plan for everything, and every
   thing combined to keep creation alive.
If creation is so complex and is planned, he
   thought, then someone must have made it so.
As everything is created to exist in harmony and
   peace, then Whoever created must be
   benevolent and kind.

Then he started to understand this must be God,
   this must be the Creator, and that God supplies
   everything we need.
He couldn't believe he had never seen this before,
   because it is so obvious.

Mankind is like this man. He closes his eyes to
   what is obviously true, he closes his eyes to
   God's plan of creation, and closes his eyes to
   God.

One day, mankind's eyes will be opened, and then
   he will wonder why he ignored what is so
   obvious.

4/24/96

Be certain I am there,
Be sure I am with you,
Be confident I AM.

4/29/96

Love life, for it is a gift.
Live love, for it is a joy.
If you can live your life in love, you find the true joy
    that is My gift to you.

5/1/96

There was a man who thought he was strong and
    could overcome all in his life.
He relied upon himself and needed no other.
One day, he became ill and could no longer support
    himself.
In his weakness, he discovered he did need others.

There was a man who thought of himself as weak,
    as unable to do anything unless God helped
    him.
In his weakness, he would call on God to give him
    the strength to help others.

One day the two met, and the man who thought he
    was weak did all he could to help the other.
He asked God for the strength and the compassion
    to do so, for he knew it was only God Who could
    give him the strength he needed to help
    another.

The man who used to be strong, accepted the help
    offered, and when he saw how much the weaker
    man did for him, how much he helped him, and
    how the weaker man never stopped caring for
    him, he wondered where the strength came
    from.
He asked the other, "How can you do so much?
    Where do you get the energy from?"
The weaker man replied, "It is not I who has the
    strength to help you, but it is God Who gives it
    to me as a gift to share with others."

"I used to think I was strong," said the first man,
  "but now I see you have the true strength of life,
  the strength that is found in God's love. How I
  envy you now."

"Do not envy me," replied the other. "Just turn to
  God, and you will find He has enough for
  everybody. He will give to you as He gives to me,
  if you truly want it."

(*Baruch 3:14*—Learn where is wisdom, where is
  strength and understanding, that you may
  know, at the same time, where are length of
  days and life.)

5/2/96

Jesus is by your side at all times, waiting to help,
  waiting to strengthen, waiting to love.
When it is difficult, remember this, and find peace
  in Jesus.

5/2/96

Prayers in hard times are strong prayers, when you
  persevere, even though it may not seem so.

5/2/96

In the sacraments, find love.
In the sacraments, find peace.
In the sacraments, find yourself growing in My love
  and filled with My peace.

5/2/96

In the Mass, see My Son's sacrifice.
In the Mass, see My Son's gift.
In the Mass, see My Son Jesus.

(*Psalms 95:6*—Come and worship; let us bow down;
kneel before the Lord.)

5/4/96

In friendship, all is forgiven.
In friendship, all is understood.
In friendship, all is love.

5/4/96

Forgiveness, love, and understanding come with
friendship.
Be a friend to all.

5/4/96

A man who becomes a friend of all, becomes a
friend of God.
A man who becomes forgiving to all, is forgiven by
God.
A man who becomes understanding of others, finds
he is forgiven by God, Who will call him His
friend.

5/4/96

A new day dawns, the day of God's love.
A new day dawns, the day of God's mercy.
Every day is a new day where God's merciful love is
there for all.

57.

<u>5/5/96</u>

When praying is hard and you carry on, they are
 good prayers, for in your struggle you show
 your love of Me.

<u>5/7/96</u>

Persevere in prayer; find strength in the
 sacraments, and overcome with giving.

<u>5/8/96</u>

Trust brings the rewards it offers.

<u>5/8/96</u>

A son who will do whatever he is asked without
 doubt, is a true son.
A son who follows his Father's will unto the end, is
 rewarded in heaven.
A son who loves his Father so much that he will
 give anything that is asked and will see it
 through until the end, has a special place
 waiting in heaven.

<u>5/9/96</u>

Don't worry; trust.
Don't doubt; trust.
Don't fret; trust.

5/9/96

Pray, pray, pray...find your strength that way.
Love, love, love...find your help from above.
Give, give, give...find, then, the way to live.

(*Wisdom 11:21*—For your great strength is always
at your call.)

5/9/96

To trust in My love brings all you desire.
Jesus is My love, so trust in Him.

5/9/96

Praying for healing means trusting in Me.
Trust and believe, and see the wonders of My love.

(*Psalms 138:3*—The day I called for help, You heard
me.)

5/9/96

Remember in your prayers your love of God.
Remember in your prayers My love of you.
Remember in your prayers your love of Me, and find
your love comes from My love of you.

5/9/96

The Holy Spirit is there for you, waiting to answer
your prayers.
The Holy Spirit is there for all, if they ask in
humble love.
The Holy Spirit is there...always believe and accept
His will.

59.

5/12/96

Softness, gentleness, kindness, and love...always,
no matter what the situation, no matter how
difficult.
In this way, you show your love of Me.

5/12/96

Home is wherever you find the love of God.
Home is wherever you are welcomed in Jesus'
name.
Home is eternity.

5/14/96

Remember the truth always.

5/14/96

Drinking from the Cup of love means to share this
love.
Eating of the Bread of forgiveness means to offer
this forgiveness to all.
Uniting with My Son Jesus through His Body and
Blood in the Eucharist, fills you with God's love
and forgiveness, that I long to share with you.

5/17/96

Truth, honesty, humility, love...always.

5/17/96

A man one day sat looking at the lilies growing in
a field. He wondered how they could grow so
beautifully with no one to care for them; they
just grew wild in the open.
He did not understand that God cared for them and
gave them all they needed to grow and become
beautiful.

So it is with mankind, if they will open their hearts
and believe that I will supply all they need.
If they trust in Me, then mankind can grow and
become the beautiful spirits they were created
to be.

5/19/96

Thoughts of love are the only thoughts to have.
Words of love are the only words to speak.
Actions of love are the only actions to do.

When you do this, you have become My light on
earth, a light that by My grace will save so
many.

5/20/96

Life is a journey, and along the way there are so
many distractions and wrong turns placed to
stop you reaching your destination.
If you keep your heart focused on the end of the
journey, and keep to the map of life laid out by
My Son Jesus, these distractions will fade away
and you will find your destination...heaven.

61.

5/20/96

In the Bread of Life, find Jesus.
In Jesus, find life.

In the Wine of Forgiveness, find Jesus.
In Jesus, find forgiveness.

In the Bread and Wine of Communion, find Jesus'
forgiving love, which brings true life.

(*Luke 18:30*—In the world to come, eternal life.)

5/25/96

To refresh yourself, wash yourself in My Son's
Precious Blood.
To feed your spirit, eat of My Son's Body.
To find peace in your heart, become one with Jesus
in Communion.

5/26/96 (Pentecost)

Today, the church of God's Son came to be.
Today, the church full of the Holy Spirit was
formed.
Today, helped by the mother of Jesus, the apostles
became the new body of Christ.
Today, the Holy Spirit filled the hearts of men with
complete love of God...
Men who were helped by the mother of God to
accept that their fate was in God's hands, and
that Jesus would fulfill all His promises.

Today, mankind is offered the same help.
Today, the Holy Spirit waits to fill the hearts and
souls of those who will trust in God.
Today, Jesus fulfills His promise once again, by
sending the Paraclete to those who will accept
Him into their lives.

(*Romans 8:2*—The Spirit of Life in Christ Jesus has
set you free from the law of sin and death.)
(*John 16:13*—When the Spirit of Truth comes, He
will lead you to the complete truth.)
(*Timothy 2:6*—That is why I am reminding you now
to fan into a flame the gift that God gave you.)

5/26/96

A wife, a husband, one in My eyes.
A family united in love, My love.
A bond between man, woman, and God...a bond
that never should be broken.

(*Ecclesiasticus 19:20*—Wisdom is entirely
constituted by the fulfilling of the law.)

5/27/96

As faith grows, so do the gifts.

5/27/96

Patience, peace, prayer.
In prayer, find the peace that brings patience.

5/31/96

A son who loves, is a true son.
A son who forgives, is a loving son.
A son who understands what weaknesses are and
forgives them in love, is a son of Mine.

My love, My heart, My Son Jesus.
My joy, My happiness, My Son Jesus.
My forgiveness, My hope, My Son Jesus.
My Son Jesus, Who loves everyone from deep within
His heart, brings joy and happiness to those
who accept His forgiveness, and hope for a
better future in God.

6/6/96

To trust and wait, then to accept, is a sign of faith.
To love and worship, then to do, is a sign of faith.
To give and give, then give again, is a sign of faith.

6/6/96

Those who show patience, show they care for
others.
Those who show understanding, show they are
concerned for others.
Those who show a patient understanding, show
they love others.

6/6/96

Love shines through; love overcomes; love
triumphs,
Love, just love.

6/6/96

In service, love.
In service, live.
In service, live eternally in love.

6/6/96

When you look into a river, you see the salmon
struggling to reach their final destination, a
destination that will mean the end of their life,
but also a new beginning of life in the young
they spawn.

Think of how men struggle in this life and how,
when they reach their final destination, it can
bring life out of death.

The difference in the salmon is that they die and
new salmon are born.
With men, they die to be reborn into eternal life
with God.

The struggle...so similar, the rewards...so different.

6/7/96

My Son looks upon mankind and sees each heart as
His brother or sister, each soul as His family,
and each person as His child.
What love has Jesus...enough for everyone and still
more.

6/7/96

It is better to wait in love, than to hurry in
blindness.
Everything comes to those who wait.

6/9/96

Look at the clouds in the sky, the water in the
    rivers and oceans, and the earth on the ground.
So different, yet all with a purpose, and all from
    Me.

Look at animals on the land, the birds in the air,
    and the fish in the sea.
So different, yet all with a purpose, and all from
    Me.

Look at the differences and see the necessity for
    each, how together they support each other.

This is how it is with mankind: so many differences,
    yet all from Me, all there to support and help
    each other.

This is creation.

6/10/96

The thoughts of men can be thoughts of good or
    bad.
The thoughts of men can be influenced by good or
    bad.
The thoughts of men can become good or bad;
    the choice is man's.

When evil thoughts are harbored, evil happens.
When good thoughts are welcomed, good happens.
A simple choice, but a choice so hard to make.

When bad thoughts are in your mind, think of good.
When good thoughts are in your mind, act on them.
Goodness, from God.
Evil, a rejection of God.
An obvious choice.
Choose wisely, and know what you choose.

6/11/96

I am, I was, and I always will be.
Words hard to understand, but in them a
  description of God.
I am, now.
I was, always.
I will be forever.

I exist.
I am existence.
I am forever.

I was in the beginning.
I am the beginning.
I am the end.
I am God.

(*Isaiah 47:10*—I, and none besides Me.)

6/13/96

As you walk the path of life, remember that those
  you meet are walking the same path.
It is just that sometimes they do not follow the
  directions that keep them on the correct way...
The way of Jesus.

6/17/96

It is natural to worry about your children, for this
  is part of being human.
The concern in parents' hearts shows the depth of
  their love, a love I first put there.

6/19/96

To be a son of Mine, love.
Love Me, your God; love your fellow man, and love
all that I have created.
When you do this, then you show you are My
family.

6/24/96

Prayer in the morning.
Prayer in the daytime.
Prayer in the night.
Pray always, and grow.

6/28/96

As you walk with Me, be humble.
As you talk for Me, be humble.
As you give for Me, be humble.

Humility, a gift of love you can offer Me, for in
humility you show you truly love Me.

6/29/96

Sharing love, giving love, growing love.

6/29/96

Friendship in God, the only friendship that is true.

6/29/96

It is the truth that always wins.
Deceit eventually is found out.
It may not be immediate, but it is always
    discovered.

Deceit changes good to bad; deceit hardens hearts,
    and deceit only brings pain.

All those who live in deceit, must accept the truth,
    or they may be lost forever.

6/30/96

To wonder about the path ahead is understandable,
    for who wouldn't?
To worry about the path ahead is unnecessary, for
    worry will not change anything.

6/30/96

To save a soul is one of the greatest gifts I offer,
    and I offer it through My Son Jesus.

(2 *Maccabees 3:31*—To bestow life on a man lying
    on the very point of death.)

7/1/96

Underneath the outer layers of mankind is a
  deep-seated love, the love that I gave man.
To find this love today is difficult, because more
  and more layers of sin cover it.
Sometimes it is sin so sublime, mankind does not
  recognize it.

As these layers grow, the hearts of men become
  colder, and so more sin is accepted and the
  layers grow even more.
One day, if mankind does not change, many will
  have covered this love completely, and then it
  will be hard for them to remove it.

My Son Jesus offers all the opportunity to cleanse
  the soul and let this love shine through once
  more.
So, turn to Jesus and turn to love, love that will see
  you live forever.

(*Ezekiel 14:6*—The Lord Yahweh says this: come
  back, renounce your idols, and give up all your
  filthy practices.)

7/4/96

Give thanks to those who help.
Give praise to those who give.
Give glory only to God.

7/4/96

Friends in God.
Friends in love.
Friends in eternity.

7/5/96

Truth overcomes evil.
Light overcomes dark.
Hope overcomes despair.

I am the truth that brings hope through My Son
Jesus, Who, with the Holy Spirit, shines light
into the dark.

7/7/96

Humility is a virtue that leads you to opening your
heart in complete obedience to Me.
With humility comes the understanding of your true
place in creation and your reason for being.
It is to love your God and to help your brothers and
sisters come closer to Me.

In humility you ask for nothing, as you know I will
supply what you need, and in humility you
accept what I give to you.

Be humble and be strong.

7/7/96

To admire a thing of beauty is to admire what I
created.
As I have created all, see the beauty in everything.

7/7/96

Never prejudge; always wait to see what is, before
making a judgment.

71.

<u>7/7/96</u>

In hope, receive My Son's Body.
In love, receive My Son's Blood.
In union with Jesus, bring My love to those who
    search without hope.
My love is Jesus, and Jesus is the only hope.
Bring Jesus to all.

<u>7/10/96</u>

Pray from the heart.

<u>7/12/96</u>

My Son Jesus has shown mankind how life is
    supposed to be lived.
Jesus went through much hardship and suffering in
    His life, but through all that, He still loved His
    brothers and sisters on earth...all of them.
Jesus overcame His human side, and showed how it
    is the spiritual life that is most important.

Jesus also showed that the body is there for man
    to grow in love and spirituality. That the body is
    an integral part of the growth of the whole
    being, and that controlling your body brings you
    spiritual strength, but when your body controls
    you, it brings spiritual weakness.
Jesus at times showed His struggle with His
    humanity, but by example taught that through
    humility and love, temptations can be overcome.

Jesus set a clear path for all to walk by walking it
    Himself, and showing that all can be overcome
    if you trust in God.

(*Habakkuk 1:5*—For I am doing something in your
    days.)

7/12/96

It is wise to be careful in what you say, for a foolish
tongue even with good intentions, may bring
unnecessary difficulties.

7/12/96

Be wise in what you say; be kind in what you do;
be generous in what you give, and then be a
reflection of My Son Jesus.

7/15/96

All around you are angels protecting you and
guiding you.
Trust in My angels, and know you are safe in their
arms.

7/17/96

My Son leads you to heaven.
My Son leads you to eternal life.
My Son leads you to Me.
My Son Jesus leads you to heaven to enjoy eternal
life with Me.

(*Ecclesiasticus 29:14*—Place thy treasure in the
commandments of the Most High, and it shall
bring thee more profit than gold.)

7/17/96

Friendship does not depend on wealth, only on love.

73.

On the earth are many different people, different
   races, different colors, different creeds.
So many differences, yet all are so much the same.

All seek security in life; all seek enough to eat,
   enough to survive; all seek love, and all seek
   happiness.

How sad it is that the differences cannot be put
   aside to allow the similarities to unite and join
   mankind in love.

United, mankind can bring peace and prosperity
   to the world.
Divided, only pain and suffering.

7/21/96

Peace of mind is found in love, My love.

7/26/96

In your heart, hold true to My commandments.
In your heart, hold true to My love.
In your heart, hold true to God and find that the
   commandments I have given are a sign of My
   love.

(Psalms 112:1—Happy the man who fears Yahweh,
   by joyfully keeping His commandments.)

7/28/96

Distractions will always be before you.
Find the strength to overcome, in prayer and the
   sacraments.

7/29/96

My Son gave His life for mankind.
In return, all He asks is love.
So much given by My Son and so little asked in
    return.

7/30/96

In God you trust.
In God you love.
In God you serve.
Your service for Me shows how much you love Me
    and how deep is your trust.

(*Judith 12:6*—Let my Lord kindly give orders for
    your servant to be allowed to go out and pray.)

7/31/96

The Holy Spirit fills the hearts of those who love
    God.
The Holy Spirit fills the souls of those who work for
    God.
The Holy Spirit fills the lives of those who praise
    God.
Filled with the Spirit, all is possible.

8/1/96

The joy of seeing My love in action is the joy of love.
Let that joy fill you, and see My love grow in you.

(*Isaiah 66:14*—At the sight, your heart will rejoice.)

8/1/96

Jesus is a friend to all.
Jesus is the Savior for all.
Jesus is God of all.

8/1/96

Open hearts, waiting to be filled with love.
Open hearts, waiting to be guided in love.
Open hearts. existing in love.

This is how mankind should be, open to Me.

(*Isaiah 5:1*—Let me sing to my friend the song of
His love.)

8/1/96

To do the right thing in all you do, is to do what I
ask.

8/1/96

Friendship, love, and goodness all go together, for
when you are friends in God, there is love and
goodness in what you do.

8/3/96

In spiritual life, human life becomes complete.

(*Proverbs 11:2*—The blessing of the Lord, it maketh
rich.)

8/5/96

A prayerful life,
A sacramental life,
A loving life, is a full life.

8/5/96

In the Mass, find love.
In the Mass, find peace.
In the Mass, find hope.
For Jesus brings His love to you in the Eucharist
    which, if you accept, will bring you peace of
    heart and hope in life.

(*Isaiah 15:27*—For the Lord of Hosts hath purposed
and who shall disannul it?)

8/8/96

Graces are granted through the Trinity Rosary for
    those in purgatory.
Graces are granted through the Trinity Rosary for
    those who suffer.
Graces are granted through the Trinity Rosary for
    those who want to come closer to God.
The Trinity Rosary, a meditation on God, that offers
    so many graces to those who pray it.

8/10/96

Friendship means understanding.
Friendship means caring.
Friendship means loving.
Jesus is your friend Who understands all you need,
    and in His love, cares for you.

(*Hosea 2:23*—I will love the unloved.)

77.

To share My love, is your work.
To share My gifts, is your duty.
To want to share is your choice, a choice of love
that can be a gift for all.

8/10/96

The joy of knowing Me, is the joy of love.

(*Isaiah 5:1*—Let me sing to my friend the song of
His love.)

8/10/96

The gifts I give to you, I give for the good of all,
so you must give to all.
When you do this, I will give you more and more,
so in turn, you can give more.

8/12/96

There is a place in My heart for all people.
There is a place in My heart for everyone.
There is a place in My heart for those who seek it.
Seek and you shall find.

8/12/96

Concern for others is part of loving Me, but in that
concern, do not offend others.
Love them as well.

8/13/96

The Bread of life is offered to mankind in every
     Eucharist.
The Blood of salvation is offered to mankind in
     every sacrament of Communion.
The food of eternal joy is offered to mankind in
     every celebration of love in the Mass.

Eat of My Son, Jesus, and be filled with love.
Drink of My Son, Jesus, and be washed in joy.
Unite with My Son, Jesus, and live forever.

(*John 15:5*—Whoever remains in Me, with Me in
     him, bears fruit in plenty.)

8/13/96

Be an example to others of how to live: truthfully,
     lovingly, and kindly.

8/21/96

Be humble in all you do, for in humility, you open
     the hearts of others to My love.

8/23/96

In life, love, and in love, live.
I am love, and through Me, find true life.

8/24/96

The world needs love.
The world needs hope.
The world needs peace.
All the needs of the world are found in My Son
     Jesus, for He is all the world needs.

8/24/96

In creation, I give all to mankind for its existence
and for its growth in Me.
Creation is My gift, and so all of creation should be
loved, as it is created in and from love.

8/30/96

Mary, My daughter, Queen of Prophets, servant of
God, humble maid, an example of how to live for
and with God.
An example to follow, and a mother to turn to
for love and for help.

8/30/96

The Commandments should be kept by all.
The Commandments given to Moses and given by
Jesus.
The Commandments are the way to live.

(*Jonah 3:3*—In obedience to the word of Yahweh.)

9/1/96

My love reaches out to touch all hearts.
My love reaches out to fill all hearts.
My love reaches out to unite all hearts.
My love is Jesus, and Jesus reaches out to all in
love.

(*Psalms 136:16*—His love is everlasting.)

9/2/96

The strength of love found in the sacraments can
  help all defeat the sin in their lives.
The strength of love found in the sacraments can
  heal all of their afflictions.
The strength of love found in the sacraments can
  help all to live happy and joyful lives.
The sacraments...gifts of love for all to find strength
  in.

(Isaiah 57:10—Finding your strength revived, you
  never weakened.)

9/3/96

Through adversity, love.
Through difficulties, love.
Through hard times, love.
Love, always love.

9/4/96

Into My arms, place your troubles.
Into My arms, place your cares.
Into My arms, place yourself, and see your prayers
  answered, your needs fulfilled, and your life
  complete.

9/6/96

Demands should never be made of others, only
  requests.
Demands may hurt; requests encourage.
Demands confront; requests consider the feelings
  of others.

(Isaiah 21:12—If you want to, why not ask?)

81.

9/9/96

Joy in life,
Joy in love,
Joy in God.
Life becomes a joy, when you are in love with God.

(*Proverbs 8:32*—Happy those who keep My ways.)

9/11/96

To be part of My family, you only have to
    want to be.
To be part of My family, you only have to love Me.
To be part of My family, you only have to accept
    My love.
My family will live in love forever, and enjoy the
    rewards of heaven in eternity.
I offer this to all who accept My love in their lives.

(*Isaiah 44:23*—Shout for joy, you heavens, for
    Yahweh has been at work. Shout aloud, you
    earth below.)

9/11/96

Pray with love.
Pray in faith.
Pray for good, and see your prayers answered.

9/12/96

As My Son suffered, so did I.
As My Son forgave, so did I.
As My Son redeemed, so did I.

My Son, One with Me.
My Son, united in My heart.
My Son, filled with My Spirit.

My Son, God.
My Son, Jesus.
My Son, Love.

(*Jonah 2:10*—But I, with a song of praise, will
sacrifice to you. The vow I have made, I will
fulfill. Salvation comes from Yahweh.)

9/12/96

Money can be a source of joy when it is used for
good, or misery when it is used for evil.

9/12/96

In war, many are filled with madness.
In war, many become servants of sin.
In war, many become blind to the truth.

War, a burden that often is welcomed by many.
War, a burden that often is seen as exciting by
many.
War, a burden that often is shouldered by many
more than those who take part in it.

War, always to be avoided, but so often welcomed
by those who are blinded by the excitement of
war, a blindness that really is a madness that
drags many into the service of sin.

(*Isaiah 38:18*—Death does not extol You. Those who
go down to the pit, do not go on trusting in Your
faithfulness.)

83.

9/13/96

As the sun shines so brightly in the sky, so shines
the love of My Son Jesus upon mankind.
As the sun lights up the sky, so My Son's love lights
up the hearts of those who accept Him as Lord.
As the sun radiates warmth for plants to grow and
all to live by, so My Son radiates love into the
souls of those who seek Him.

Through My Son Jesus, all can find the warmth of
love that lights up their hearts and helps them
grow closer to God.

(*Ecclesiasticus 46:2*—How splendid was He, when
He raised His arms.)

9/13/96

Prayers open your heart.
Prayers open your soul.
Prayers open the door to heaven.

9/15/96

The face of love, the face of Jesus.
The face of mercy, the face of Jesus.
The face of God, the face of Jesus.

9/16/96

Strength is found in prayer.
Peace is found in the sacraments.
Love is found in Me.

9/16/96

The love of My Son is found in the celebration
of the Eucharist.

9/18/96

In your sleep, find peace.
In your sleep, find love.
In your sleep, find comfort.
When you sleep peacefully, you sleep in My love,
which comforts your soul and refreshes your
body.

9/19/96

In trust, all is possible.
In love, all can be.
In God, all is.

9/20/96

A man is made of spirit as well as flesh.
Many look after and treat their bodies well, but
many ignore their spirit.
To strengthen and grow spiritually, find your needs
fulfilled in the sacraments and prayer.
The sacraments—spiritual food and spiritual
sweetness. Prayer—spiritual exercises to
strengthen and grow.

9/20/96

Belief comes from truth.

9/22/96

Take your strength from the sacraments.
Find your peace in prayer.
See that nothing can take you from My love, and be
at peace.

(*Psalms 84:11*—The Lord is our protector and King.)

9/22/96 *(During a visit to New Zealand)*

New Zealand, land of hope.
New Zealand, land of peace.
New Zealand, land of seekers.
In New Zealand many search for peace, all hope for
prosperity, and some seek Me.
If all could seek Me, their search would end and
their hopes would be realized.

9/22/96

Trust in God is a wonderful gift; keep trusting.

9/24/96

Show love to all, and show God to all.

9/26/96

In My heart is all that mankind could ever desire.
In My heart is everything that is best for mankind.
In My heart is an all embracing love that contains
everything that man could ever desire, and all
that is needed for its very existence.
In My Heart is Jesus.

9/28/96

Life can be a joy or a misery.
Life can be exciting or dull.
Life can be fulfilled or empty.
In Jesus, the joy of life is found as your every
    moment is filled with the excitement of His love.

9/29/96

My Son came to forgive.
My Son came to show mercy.
My Son came to offer love.

His love is there for everyone.
His mercy is offered to all.
His forgiveness is a gift to all.

Those who accept His offering will receive in love
    His gift, and enjoy eternal peace.

(*Psalms 45:1*—My heart is stirred by a noble theme.)

9/29/96

A troubled heart can be soothed with love.

9/30/96

Truth is placed within each heart.
Truth, however, is often covered with pride and
    with self.
Truth is still within each heart...it only needs to be
    released by overcoming oneself in humility.

9/30/96

It is a foolish generation that ignores the truth.

10/1/96

Humility shows your love for Me.
Humility shows your praise of Me.
Humility shows your thanks to Me.

10/1/96

In love be kind,
In love be gentle,
In love be giving; then you live in Me.

10/4/96

As I look upon creation, I see the love, the joy, the
    happiness I created.
As I look upon creation, I see how mankind is often
    blinded to what is given.
As I look upon creation, I see the future that can be
    all of mankind's.

10/4/96

Pride is a weight upon your soul.
Humility, a refreshing breeze that blows the burden
    of pride away.
Love, a gift that can fill you with humility, if you
    remove your pride and see what is offered in
    love.

10/4/96

Human weaknesses can be overcome by trusting in
  Me.
Thoughts of self can be overcome by loving Jesus.
The glory of God can be seen when you overcome
  yourself and your weaknesses, by trusting in Me
  and showing your love of My Son Jesus.

10/6/96

To rest in prayer is a grace many forget.
To rest in prayer, be silent with me, My Son, and
  My Spirit, and allow God's strength to refresh.
To rest in prayer is so important for spiritual
  growth, for it is in this rest, you give yourself
  time to hear Me.

(*Proverbs 3:1*—My Son, forget not my teaching.)

10/6/96

To love God is a gift that is offered to all.
To love God is a gift that offers all.
To love God is a gift that is all.

(*Isaiah 66:14*—When you see this, your heart shall
  rejoice.)

10/6/96

Pride, a destroyer of souls; humility, a savior of
  souls.

89.

10/11/96

Around the world are many lost souls, who need to
   hear the truth of God.
Around the world are many confused souls, who
   need to know the love of God.
Around the world are many distressed souls, who
   need to feel the peace of God.

In Jesus, My Son, they can find all they need, but
   they need to be told the truth in love, so that
   the peace of God can be theirs.

(2 Machabees 1:4—May He open your heart in His
   law and in His commandments, and send you
   peace.)

10/11/96

To look in love, means to look from your heart.
To look in love, means to see with eyes of
   forgiveness.
To look in love, means to look kindly upon those
   who suffer.

Love, the only way to look.
Love, the only way to act.
Love, the only reason for life.

10/11/96

A family that loves, cannot be broken.
A family that prays, cannot be divided.
A family that loves God and prays for God's love,
   can only grow and will find its eternal reward
   in heaven.

(Jeremiah 32:38—And they shall be My people, and
   I will be their God.)

10/11/96

A commandment is not to be broken, regardless of
    the reason.
A commandment must be kept, for this is the
    reason it was given.
A commandment can never be changed, for it is the
    Word of God.

10/16/96

My Son Jesus looks over the world of mankind with
    love, and offers forgiveness to all.
Mankind only needs to look to Jesus, and ask for it.

10/16/96

Be kind always.
Be forgiving always.
Be loving always.
Every way you can forgive,
Every way you can love,
Every way you can show kindness, then every way
    be a reflection of Jesus.

10/17/96

Freedom of speech does not mean freedom to abuse
    others.
Freedom of movement does not mean walking over
    others.
Freedom of religion does not mean accepting others'
    beliefs which are away from God.
Freedom is only found in My love, for in My love
    you are free of all concerns, all cares, all anger,
    all hate, all evil, all.
In My love, your freedom is guaranteed for eternity.

(*Sirach 39:22*—His blessing overflows like the Nile.)

91.

10/18/96

Each day a gift,
Each moment a joy,
Each heartbeat a gift of love that brings joy.

This is how life should be.

10/18/96

Be joyful in love,
Be happy in love,
Be at peace in love.

In My love, there is the peace of God that fills you
    with happiness and makes life a joy.

(*Isaiah 12:3*—With joy you will draw water at the
    fountain of salvation.)

10/18/96

A confused mind needs only to see My love for all to
    become clear.

(*Wisdom 2:14*—To us, he is a censure of our
    thoughts.)

10/19/96

Let patience be your way.
Let love be your strength.
Let God be your life.

In Me, find your life complete.
In love, let your life be strengthened.
In patience, follow the way that is life.

10/19/96

The joy of sharing My love should be your reward.

10/23/96

My heart is full of love,
My heart is full of joy,
My heart is full of happiness, and I offer this to all
    hearts that love Me.

10/23/96

A Father's love,
A Son's love,
A Spirit of love...there in the Trinity.

10/26/96

Take My love to those you meet.
Take My forgiveness to those you meet.
Take My Son to those you meet in the world, and
    tell them of My forgiving love, which is Jesus.

(*Jeremiah 15:19*—If you repent, so that I restore
    you, in My presence you shall stand.)

10/27/96

A restful day,
A peaceful day,
A God-filled day...
The Sabbath.

10/27/96

A man one day was offered a gift from a friend.
Not wishing to offend his friend, even though he
    had no need of the gift, he accepted it.
A short while later he met another friend who was
    in need of what he had received from his friend,
    and so the man gave it to the one in need.
Afterwards the man wondered if he had hurt the
    first friend by giving away this gift.

One day again, he met this friend who knew that
    the gift had been passed on.
The friend was happy that someone in need had
    been helped by his first action.
The man was happy when his friend explained this
    to him saying, "A gift given in love has no
    restrictions or expectations, only the hope that
    it can be useful. My gift was accepted in love so
    that makes me happy, but I am even happier
    that, in love, you opened your heart and shared
    my gift of love with another who needed it."

Always remember, give to those in need and always
    give in love, and when you receive gifts, see they
    are there to be shared.

10/28/96

Become a brother to all you meet, become part of
    their family and make them part of yours, for
    you all come from the same Father.

10/28/96

The freedom of love is the only freedom you need,
    for in love all is a joy.

10/28/96

In love enjoy life, in life enjoy love.

10/28/96

In your life, enjoy each moment for the gift of love it
is that I give to you, and in love bring each
moment alive.

10/29/96

A son who loves his Father is treasured and
rewarded by his Father.
A son who offers all to his Father will, in return,
receive all that is needed in his life.
A son who worships his Father is a pleasing sight to
his Father, who will keep a special place in his
heart for his son.

10/29/96

Speak of love,
Speak in love,
Speak with love
Then speak for Me.

10/29/96

In My daughter Mary's heart is a love for all
mankind, a love all mankind should try to
imitate, a love that is pure, a love that is an
example of how mankind was created to be.

10/30/96

Love overcomes confusion.
Love overcomes concerns.
Love overcomes all, so always love.

11/1/96

Saints in heaven rejoice in My love.
Saints in heaven exist in My love.
Saints in heaven reach out to mankind in My love.
The saints in heaven reach out to mankind, and will
     rejoice when mankind returns to exist in My
     love for eternity.

11/2/96

Souls need prayer,
Souls need love,
Souls need forgiveness.
With the grace your prayers bring, souls can be
     forgiven and come to My eternal love.

11/3/96

In the elderly is the beauty of age.
In the elderly is the wisdom of years.
In the elderly is the understanding of life.
The elderly are there to guide the young, to advise
     the following generations, and there as part of
     your family.

11/6/96

A son of Mine reflects My love.
A son of Mine shares My kindness.
A son of Mine gives, always gives, in My name.

11/6/96

Feel My love within, then know it is I.

11/6/96

Rest brings peace of mind,
Rest brings peace of heart,
Rest brings peace of spirit, when you rest in Me.

11/6/96

Evil can never win, for it was defeated by My Son's
    sacrifice on the cross.
When mankind comes to terms with this and
    accepts it, evil will disappear from their hearts.

11/8/96

Mankind, a creation of love.
Love, a gift to mankind.

11/8/96

Miracles do happen.
Miracles are possible.
Miracles are My gifts to heal My children, and bring
    them home to Me.

11/9/96

In the Word of God, is life.
In the Word of God, is love.
In the Word of God, is eternity.
Jesus is the Word.

97.

11/9/96

Humanity has its weaknesses, weaknesses which
can be overcome if humanity really wants.
The strength to overcome is found in humble
acceptance of My love and My will.
With this, mankind will overcome its pride and its
self, the weaknesses that lead mankind from
Me.

11/14/96

When fruit is ripe, it is sweet to the taste.
When souls are grown in love, they are sweet to see.
When souls full of love do My work, they bear much
fruit and the sweetness of love grows.

11/17/96

Truth, honesty, integrity always.
Never be anything else, and never accept anything
else.
Forgiveness, love, and compassion always, and be a
reflection of Jesus.
Hope, trust, and believe always, and be rewarded in
heaven.

(Psalms 26:11—But as for me, I walk in my
integrity: redeem me, and be gracious to me.)

11/19/96

The fear of God comes when you live away from
God, and the love of God comes when you live in
God.
The love of God is Jesus, so live in Jesus.
The fear of God is self-imposed when you live in sin,
so live away from sin, and find My love awaiting
in My Son Jesus.

11/19/96

Gifts given in love should be accepted in love and, when possible, shared with others.

11/19/96

Working in love and from the heart, makes work a joy.

11/23/96

Jesus stands by your side with understanding and with love.
Jesus lives in your heart with joy and with love.
Jesus fills your soul with graces and with love.
My Son surrounds you, fills you, and loves you, so that you, too, now become a true son of God.

(2 *Timothy* 2:12—If we endure, we will also reign with Him.)

11/28/96

If you look upon another with desires of self, then you look in sin.
If you look upon another with desires for their good, then you look in love.
If you look upon another with desires of bringing My love to them, then this selfless act becomes a grace in which you can grow.

11/28/96

In the face of others, see My love.
In the heart of others, see My joy.
In the spirit of others, see My hope.

99.

<u>12/5/96</u>

Wisdom means understanding.
Wisdom means caring.
Wisdom means forgiveness,
For without these there is no wisdom.

(*Isaiah 5:21*—Woe to those who think themselves
wise and believe themselves cunning.)

<u>12/10/96</u>

A sense of humor is a gift of God, but like all gifts it
can be used for good or it can be misused.
When it is used for good, it can bring joy to many.
When it is misused, it can bring sadness to some.

<u>12/15/96</u>

Love is needed in times of sickness.
Care is needed in times of ill health.
Attention is needed in times of distress.

(*2 Chronicles 15:4*—But in their distress, they will
return to Yahweh, the God of Israel.)

<u>12/17/96</u>

There is no rest for the wicked, but there is eternal
rest for the good.

12/19/96

A boy one day started to steal and he got away with
    it, so he stole more and more.
Soon he would steal anything he could from family,
    from friends, and even from the church.

As he grew, he became a drinker, a fighter, a liar,
    and a sinner.
His friends never condemned him, only encouraged
    him.
His family tried to stop him sinning, but he would
    not listen.

Now he was a man, and he met a woman he loved;
    they married and had a family, but still he
    sinned, still he would not listen.
His wife tried to change him, but he ignored her
    pleas and got worse; more violence, more
    alcohol, more sinning.
He tried to please only his friends and his pride.

Many became afraid of him, many became admirers
    of him, and many became ashamed of him.
He did not care.
If others annoyed him, he would hurt them; if
    others disagreed with him, he would ignore
    them; and if others opposed him, he would
    ridicule them.

A man of pride and of sin, but within this man was
    a softness, a gentleness, which he did not show
    often.
Within this man was a feeling of helping the
    downtrodden.
Within this man was a wanting the world to change.
The man within did not often surface, but when he
    did, it surprised even himself.

One day this man thought he was going to die.
One day he wondered if he was going mad.
One day he decided to change.

The times of death came close so many times, as he
struggled to rid himself of the evil he had
embraced.

Within his heart, unknown to him, was a longing
for God, and as he tried to overcome evil, this
longing grew and grew.

God reached out and touched his heart, giving him
the strength to persevere.

God sent His angels and His saints to help in the
battle that was taking place for this man's soul.

The evil one tried harder to destroy this man with
threats to him, his family, and his friends.

The evil one intensified his attacks trying to
frighten, trying to kill, trying to destroy this
man and his growing faith.

God sent His merciful mother to walk with this
man, to bring him closer to God, to strengthen
his love of God.

This man fell in love with the mother of God, his
mother.

This man longed to please her, longed to give her
little gifts of love in his prayers and in his life.

Satan did not stop, and yet this man, who used to
be so deep in sin, rejected Satan and turned his
back on evil completely.

This angered the evil one, who still tried to hurt, to
frighten, and to kill this man.

Then one day God, Himself, came in the form of
Jesus, His Son.

Jesus offered forgiveness and love, and the man,
even though he did not know why this would
happen to him, reached out to Jesus and
embraced His love.

Jesus led this man to understand how his life had
been wasted, and how he now had the
opportunity to do good, to help people by doing
God's work.

Without hesitation, without any demands, and with
complete acceptance of God's will, this man
accepted what Jesus asked.

Soon the Holy Spirit filled this man with gifts and
graces to take to the world.
Soon I, My Son, and the Holy Spirit asked this man
to step out in faith, and in love he did.

This man makes many mistakes and makes many
problems for himself, but through all this, he
loves God and completely obeys God's will.
This man thinks little of himself, and often only
sees the mistakes he makes, and not the good
he does by God's grace.
This man sees himself as being too proud, too
selfish, too greedy, too judgmental, too
unforgiving, and too jealous of others.
This man sees now what he was blind to in the
past; now he magnifies what is small, where in
the past he shrunk what was large.

Now he cannot bear to sin or offend God, where
before it meant little.
Now he prays and prays, where before his prayers
were few.
Now he sees the truth of the sacraments, where
before he never really saw them.
Now he tries his hardest to do God's will, where
before it was only his own will.

So much goodness now, but this man cannot see it
in himself, just as before he could not see the
evil.

103.

12/19/96

The Trinity,
The divine mystery...
One God, yet three Persons.

Remember all is possible in Me.

(*Isaiah 48:16*—From the beginning.)

12/27/96

Each day can be a prayer of love offered to Me.
Each day can be an appreciation of the gift I give to
    you.
Each day can be a sign of your love for Me.

(*Matthew 24:50*—His master will come on a day he
    does not expect.)

12/30/96

Friends long to be with each other.
Friends long to hear each other.
Friends long to see each other.
Be a friend to all, and be a friend of Mine.

1/3/97

Today find peace in your heart.
Today find forgiveness in your heart.
Today find love in your heart.
It is when you are forgiven and you learn to forgive
    others that you find peace, as your heart grows
    in love.

(*Psalms 71:23*—And this soul of mine, which You
    have redeemed.)

1/5/97

When you pray, I am listening,
When you pray, I am there,
When you pray, I am waiting on each word.
Pray from your heart, and I will take your words
into My heart.

(*Psalms 77:1*—Loudly I cry to God, loudly to God,
Who hears me.)

1/6/97

It is under difficult circumstances that you show
how strong is your love for Me.

1/8/97

My Son, Jesus, came to earth to bring peace, love,
and forgiveness.
To follow Jesus, you must keep these in your heart,
for this is His way.

1/17/97

Within your heart is the strength you seek.
Within your heart is the love you desire.
Within your heart is the Son of God, Who, by His
love, gives you the strength you need to
overcome all evil.

(*Lamentations 1:13*—He has sent a fire from on
high.)
(*2 Timothy 2:1*—Accept the strength, my dear son,
that comes from the grace of Jesus Christ.)

1/19/97

Please Me, not man.

1/24/97

The joy you find in My love is a joy all can have...
Tell them.

(*Isaiah 2:5*—Come, let us walk in the light of
Yahweh.)

1/25/97

Faith is like a river; when there are no blockages, it
flows freely.
Place a dam in the river and it stops or slows its
flow.
Sin is the blockage that can stop your faith; prayer
is a way of breaking the dam, so that your faith
can flow freely.

(Psalms 25:8—He teaches the way to sinners.)

1/26/97

The Sabbath keep holy,
The Sabbath keep true,
The Sabbath keep in love, and find true holiness.

(*Psalms 118:1*—Give thanks to Yahweh, for He is
good.)

1/26/97

Worshipping God is a grace I give to all mankind, a grace that many do not understand, a grace that will bring all that is needed to mankind for all to live at peace and in love.

(*Daniel 3:32*—May peace be always with you.)

1/31/97

In the time you spend with Me, empty your mind of all else and make Me your thoughts.

(*1Maccabees 2:61*—All who hope in Him will not be found to falter.)

2/3/97

Be strong in love,
Be strong in faith,
Be strong in humility; then all will know you are Mine.

(*2 Chronicles 36:18*—And the treasures of the house of the Lord.)

2/7/97

Many seek to do My will, but many confuse their will with Mine.

107.

2/10/97

Around My throne in heaven, are millions upon
    millions of angels and saints, waiting to serve
    Me in love.
Each one waits to do My will, and waits to help in
    the victory over evil, the victory which My Son
    Jesus has already won.

Each angel and saint longs to save those souls that
    are leaving My love and entering the realms of
    darkness.
Each angel and saint, by the power of My love, has
    the grace to do so, when I ask.
Each angel and saint looks to earth and hopes they
    will have the opportunity to help, an
    opportunity that can be theirs, when a soul on
    earth turns to Me and asks for My love and My
    help.

When this happens, I will send My servants of love
    to answer the prayers of man.
My servants will be filled with joy at the chance to
    save a soul and to do My will.

Remember, if you ask, I will answer...and when I
    answer, remember to thank the angels and
    saints who come to help you in My love.

(*Luke 4:11*—On their hands, they will bear you up.)

2/10/97

Time to Me is eternity,
Time to Me is forever,
Time to Me is never-ending.
In time, you can find an eternity of love and be
    forever in love with Me in a never-ending joy.

(*Isaiah 34:17*—They shall possess it forever.)

2/16/97

March on, do not look back.
In battle, if you look back you are lost; look forward
and keep fighting in My love, then you cannot
be defeated, for the power of God is with you.

(*Matthew 16:18*—And the gates of Hades will not
prevail against it.)

2/17/97

Love is an expression of self.
If you show love and live love, then this is what you
become.

2/19/97

Looking into a stream, you see the water flowing
over the stones beneath.
Looking into the heart of Jesus, you see the living
water flowing over souls.
As the water in the stream makes the stones clean
and shiny, Jesus' forgiving water cleanses souls
and makes them shine.

(*Proverbs 26:23*—Like a glaze covering an earthen
vessel.)

2/20/97

The love of God unites,
The love of God builds,
The love of God strengthens.
Live in My love and be united in Me, to build and
strengthen your soul.

(*Isaiah 26:17*—Because of You, O Lord.)

109.

2/22/97

The hearts of mankind, created in love,
The hearts of mankind, created to be love,
The hearts of mankind, created as love.
Mankind should remember this and return to the
    reason for its creation...love, only love.

(*Exodus 15:13*—In Your steadfast love, You led the
people whom You redeemed.)

2/26/97

It is My church, the Catholic Church.
It is My Son's body, the Catholic Church.
It is My Spirit's gift, the Catholic Church.
The Catholic Church, the true faith of God...have
    faith in it.

(*Ezekiel 12:27*—Listen to the house of Israel.)

2/26/97

The shepherds of My Son's flock, the priests.
The shepherds of souls, the priests.
The shepherds of love, the priests.
Each priest is appointed as a shepherd, to guide
    the souls of My Son's flock deeper into My love.

(*2 Maccabees 15:12*—A good and virtuous man,
modest in appearance, gentle in manners.)

2/26/97

Full of graces,
Full of gifts,
Full of the sacraments.

Within the Church are the gifts and graces I offer
mankind, through the sacraments.

(*Isaiah 22:22*—I will place the key of the house of
David on his shoulder.)

2/26/97

Pray and pray, then see the joy in each day.

3/5/97

When your heart is full of love, your life is full of
love.

3/5/97

Try to be kind, try to be loving, and try to help
those in need. Try, just try.

3/7/97

Be at peace in My love,
Be at peace in yourself,
Be at peace in union with Me.
When you unite with My Son, you are filled with My
love, which will bring peace within yourself.

3/9/97

With nothing to hide, you have nothing to fear.
This is the importance of always being truthful.
It is only in lies that you can be defeated.

(*Jeremiah 46:27*—Do not be afraid.)

3/9/97

Recognize the love in others, then you find the love
in yourself.

(*Ecclesiasticus 21:13*—The wise man's knowledge
will increase like a flood.)

3/10/97

When you relate to other people, do it from the
heart; then they will see the truth in your
words.

(*Malachi 2:6*—The teaching of truth was in his
mouth.)

3/10/97

Do not let anger sow the seed of hate in your heart.

3/11/97

To respond in anger only leads to more suffering,
Always respond in love.

3/11/97

Suspicious minds breed broken hearts.

3/11/97

It is a hard path I know, but persevere and soon it will get easier.

(*Isaiah 32:18*—My people will live in a peaceful home.)

3/12/97

When I crowned Mary as Queen of heaven, I showed all of mankind how I rewarded someone who accepted My will completely.
When I bring the saints to heaven, again I show the rewards that can be for everyone, if they live in My love.
When I bring the martyrs to My throne in heaven where they sit in the light of My Son, I show how, if mankind is prepared to sacrifice for Me, that their place in heaven is guaranteed.

Through so many, I show the rewards of heaven and how to achieve them.

Make Mary your role model and try to live as she did; then look to the saints and martyrs to see it is possible to live this way, and to see the rewards of heaven are there for all mankind, if only they seek them.

3/12/97

When people close their hearts to God, often they cannot see it.
This is a spiritual blindness, a blindness that will cost so much.

113.

3/13/97

As I look upon the earth, I see so much sadness
    and pain, so much suffering and sin, and so
    much confusion and anger.
To overcome these, I offer My love and I offer it in
    mercy, in compassion, in understanding, and in
    forgiveness.
If love is offered in a fear-filled way, in a
    threatening way, in an angry way, in a
    demanding way, then it is not love.
How can it be?

If it is not love, then it is not of Me.

(*Psalms 118:6*—With Yahweh on my side, I fear
    nothing; what can man do to me?)

3/13/97

The joy in your heart is a reflection of My love.
Bring this joy to others, so they, too, can become a
    reflection of Me.

(*Psalms 119:81*—Keeping my hope in Your word.)

3/13/97

Working for Me is working for love, so do it in love.

(*John 4:34*—My food is to do the will of the One
    Who sent me.)

3/14/97

Would you see a man without food starve?
Would you see a man without drink thirst?
Would you see a man without love alone?

Those who do not love My Son, Jesus, are alone in
the wilderness starving and dying of thirst.

Bring them the food they need to live, bring them
the drink they need to survive, and bring them
the love they need to be saved...bring them
Jesus.

(*Hosea 11:4*—Stooping down to him, I gave him his
food.)

3/14/97

Love is hard at times, but it is worth the effort.

3/16/97

To ask a person not to sin is the right thing to do,
for how else is sin to be recognized and stopped
by those who do not know?
It is your duty to tell those you love when they do
wrong, for if you do not, then what love do you
show?

It is your duty to stand in the truth for all to see, so
that they may see an example of how to live.

Remember it is your duty as My follower, and
remember the world is full of those you love.

(*Ezekiel 36:38*—Filled with a human flock.)

115.

3/18/97

Free of the shackles of sin, mankind can grow to be spirits free in My love.

3/18/97

My Son, My love.
My Son, My offering.
My Son, My forgiveness.
In My Son, Jesus, I show the depth of My love by the forgiveness I offer to mankind.

3/18/97

Be confident in Me, and be humble in yourself.

3/21/97

My Son Jesus offers to all mankind what He offers to you: love, forgiveness, and friendship.
My Son Jesus offers to all mankind what He offers to you: an eternity in heaven.
My Son Jesus offers to all mankind what He offers to you: a chance to be redeemed.

3/21/97

Be thankful,
Be grateful,
Be hopeful.

3/23/97

A Father's hand rests upon the world, a hand of
  love and forgiveness.
Take My hand and be filled with My eternal joy
  through My Son Jesus, Who is your brother and
  Who is your Lord.

(*Micah 6:8*—And to walk humbly with your God.)

3/23/97

The sins of the flesh can be overcome by living in
  My love, for that is the only true love, and only
  goodness can exist in Me.

(*Psalms 119:1*—Happy are they whose way is
  blameless, who walk in the law of the Lord.)

3/23/97

A family is a union of love; no wonder today families
  are under attack, for evil hates love.
A family is a sign of love and stability; no wonder
  evil attacks them, for it tries to destabilize love.
A family is a way of coming closer to God, for when
  a family is built on love it is built in Me.

No wonder evil attacks families, for it tries to
  destroy what is built in Me.

Families, the building blocks of society, who, if they
  use My Son Jesus as their cornerstone, can
  never be destroyed.

(*Psalms 18:3*—Oh Lord, my rock, my fortress, my
  deliverer.)

117.

3/24/97

Stand up and proclaim the good news of My Son
   Jesus to the world...
The good news of His love.

3/24/97

Master your fears, your worries, and your concerns
   by believing in Me and that I will care for you.

3/24/97

To rest your spirit, spend time with My Son and let
   His love surround and comfort you.

3/24/97

When you look into a face of others, look with love
   and see that love reflected.

3/24/97

The battle between good and evil is waged every
   time you speak for Me.
The battle between good and evil is fought every
   time you trust in Me.
The battle between good and evil is all around you
   as you live with Me.

It is a battle in which you stand and fight for Me
   using the most powerful weapon of all...My love.

3/24/97

Humility comes with loving God, for how can you
   truly love God if you are not humble?

3/27/97

Precious moments, moments of love.
Precious moments, moments with God.
Precious moments, moments of life.

The time you live on this earth is precious and
   each moment should be spent living in the love
   of God, so that in your last moment you can
   come to God in heaven.

(*Zechariah 8:13*—So I mean to save you, for you to
   become a blessing.)

3/27/97

Patience comes to those who trust in Me.

3/27/97

A man's role in this world is to love.
A man's role in this world is to care.
A man's role in this world is to share.

Unless you do this, then you are not a true man.

(*Matthew 5:4*—Happy the gentle; they shall have the
   earth for their heritage.)

3/29/97 (Good Friday)

With Jesus' suffering, came forgiveness.
With Jesus' suffering, came hope.
With Jesus' suffering, came the offer of an eternity
   of love.
So much offered; no wonder so much was
   demanded.

(*Ezekiel 39:8*—This is the day I predicted.)

119.

3/29/97

To walk with Jesus, means to love as Jesus.

(*Proverbs 7:1*—Keep My words and treasure My
principles.)

3/29/97

The Cross, the Love, and the Forgiveness; all there
for mankind to embrace, so that it can find a
future of peace.

(*Luke 12:32*—There is no need to be afraid, little
flock, for it has pleased your Father to give you
the kingdom.)

4/2/97

The love and the joy you feel are gifts from Me to
you, gifts that are there for everyone if they
truly want them.

(*Jeremiah 23:24*—Do I not fill?)
(*Jeremiah 23:29*—Does not My Word burn like fire?)

4/2/97

Pride is the destroyer of men, for it is in pride that
sin grows.
Pride is the soil in which sin grows.
Pride is the original sin that, from generation to
generation, allows sin to grow.

(*Isaiah 58:8*—Your integrity will grow.)
(*Jeremiah 50:32*—Arrogance will stumble.)
(*Proverbs 6:15*—His fall will come.)

4/3/97

Lost souls are everywhere; help them find their
way. Tell them to love and to pray.
Lost hearts are all around; show them love and see
them found.
Lost children roam the earth; take their hands and
lead them to church.

(*Solomon 47:15*—And prepare an everlasting
sanctuary.)

4/3/97

To discover the truth, look to Jesus, for He is the
truth.

(*1 Esdra 5:2*—The Lord God of heaven.)

4/3/97

To read Holy Scripture, is to read My Word.
To understand Holy Scripture, ask of My Spirit, for
without the help of the Spirit, Holy Scripture is
impossible to comprehend.
To find in Holy Scripture the truth of God, look to
My Son's life on earth, and it is there for all to
see.

(*Tobias 14:1*—And that they be mindful of God and
bless Him at all times in truth.)

4/19/97

My Son Jesus is the rose of love, and when you love
Jesus, you share in His bouquet.

121.

My Son Jesus opens His arms to all peoples, be
  they Jew, Greek, Muslim, Hindu, Agnostic,
  Atheist, Protestant, Catholic, or any other
  creed.
My Son Jesus opens His arms to embrace all in His
  love, and to forgive all in His mercy.
My Son Jesus opens His arms to offer the way to
  heaven to all.

There is only one way, and that is through Jesus
  My Son, but, oh, so many do not understand
  this.

Tell them, and give them the opportunity of seeing
  the truth, the truth of God that is Jesus.
There is no other truth, and His truth is found in
  the sacraments and in prayer.

4/26/97

The colors of creation are a gift to mankind, so
  people can reflect upon the beauty I have given
  to them.

4/29/97

Find peace in Jesus.
Find strength in the Spirit.
Find all in Me.

4/29/97

Trusting in Me brings its reward...eternal life in
  heaven.

5/4/97

Praying is the way to come closer to Me.
The sacraments are the way to be filled with My
  gifts and graces.
Imitating and following Jesus is the way to
  holiness.

(*Ecclesiasticus 17:12*—He established an eternal
  covenant with them.)

5/4/97

Make your heart a refuge for the unloved; then find
  your heart grow in love.

(*Philippians 1:28*—United by your love for the faith
  of the Gospel.)

5/5/97

To justify sin, is to sin.
To justify wrong, is to wrong.
To justify what is wrong, makes you part of the sin
  and makes you close your heart to Me.

5/16/97

A word of love...Jesus.

5/16/97

Your trust is important,
Your faith is imperative,
Your service needed.

(*Ecclesiasticus 11:24*—And do not say, "I am self
  supporting.")

123.

The power of God,
The light of God,
The Holy Spirit.

The fire of God,
The gifts of God,
The Holy Spirit.

The grace of God,
The dove of God,
The Holy Spirit.

The Holy Spirit, One with Me and My Son, united as
the One true God, who offers the gift of love to
all.

(*Daniel 2:22*—And light dwells with Him.)

5/24/97

In a baby's eyes, are trust and love.
In a baby's eyes, are joy and hope.
In a baby's eyes, are gentleness and peace.

Become a baby in the world, and see with eyes like
these.

(*Luke 1:14*—He will be your joy and delight, and
many will rejoice at his birth.)

5/25/97

In love, life becomes a joy;
In hatred, life becomes a burden.

In love, life becomes complete;
In sin, life becomes empty.

In love, life becomes what it was meant to be;
In darkness, life becomes a drudgery.

(*Ezekiel 7:8*—I shall judge you as your conduct
deserves.)

5/25/97

When you pray for friends, remember those who are
not friendly towards you, for in your heart they,
too, should be your friends.

(*2 Maccabees 7:28*—Consider how God made them.)

5/25/97

Prayer should be from the heart, and should be an
offering of love.

(*Ephesians 1:4*—To be holy and faultless.)

5/25/97

To serve your Lord Jesus, love Him.
To love your Lord Jesus, follow Him.
To follow your Lord Jesus, glorify Him.

(*Proverbs 10:29*—The way of Yahweh.)

5/27/97

To remember one's sins is a way of defeating pride,
for when you see how weak you truly are, you
see it is only by My grace that you find the
strength to overcome evil.

(*Habakkuk 3:19*—Yahweh, my Lord, is my strength.)

5/27/97

A man of humility is a man who puts God first, and
sees others as more important than himself.

(*Isaiah 20:20*—And this will be a sign and a witness
to Yahweh.)

5/29/97

Never be demanding.
Always be grateful.

6/7/97

A man can be many things, but if he is not a man of
love, then he is empty.

(*Psalms 27:1*—Lead me on the path of integrity.)

6/7/97

When you make each person important to you, then
you make yourself in My image.

(*Mark 12:31*—You must love your neighbor as
yourself.)

6/9/97

One day a man climbed a mountain.
As he climbed, he began to lose his strength.
Each step became a struggle; each breath painful.
This man kept his eyes on the peak and persevered
    through all the pain to reach his goal.
The closer he got to the top, the more he struggled,
    the more he hurt.

At times he thought he could not go on, but within
    was a burning desire to get to the top that drove
    him on and on.
Many times he slipped and almost fell from the
    mountain, but each time he pulled himself up
    and carried on his relentless climb.

Finally, with the top a few steps away, he rested for
    a moment; as he did, a voice said, "Here, take
    my hand; let me help you."
The man looked up surprised as he saw another
    climber who had reached the top before him.
"Thank you, but how did you get here? I did not
    see you on the way up," replied the man.

"Oh, I was climbing just a little ahead of you, and I,
    too, like you, struggled to get here," said the
    climber.
"Yes, it is a hard climb," stated the man.

"But once you reach the top, it is worth it, and you
    forget the pain and suffering it took to get
    here," said the climber, as the man came to the
    top and stood beside him looking out on the
    beauty before them.
"Yes, it is worth the climb to see this," said the
    man.

Then they heard a noise and looked down to see
    another man climbing the mountain and
    struggling with his climb.

127.

Together they reached down, and said, "Here, let us
    help you with your climb. Come and join us at
    the top."
These men are like the saints in heaven who have
    overcome the mountain of sin in the world, who,
    when they reach heaven, offer their helping
    hand to those still climbing the same mountain
    they overcame.
Mankind should not be too proud to accept the help
    offered, and should turn to the saints for their
    help in reaching the beauty of heaven.

(Wisdom 19:22—Yes, Lord, you have made your
    people great and glorious. You have never failed
    to help them at any time or place.)

6/10/97

To think of My Son's Body and Blood is the greatest
    way of discerning who comes to you.

Remember that always.

(Acts 14:3—His gift of grace.)

6/14/97

The day that mankind comes to see how it truly
    lives, is the day when many will repent.
The day when mankind's sins becomes obvious to
    all, will be a day of sorrow.
The day of Jesus' return will be a day of joy and
    forgiveness for many, but not all.
Until that day, it is every Christian's duty to spread
    the good news of salvation, so that more will
    turn to Jesus on that day.

(1 Peter 2:12—Always behave honorably among
    Gentiles, so that they can see for themselves
    what moral lives you lead.)

6/17/97

The earth is a creation of My love.
The earth is a jewel of My love.
The earth is a gift of My love.

From My love, I created a jewel as a gift for
mankind, a paradise to enjoy.

Treasure this gift as you should, and see that the
jewel can shine brightly again, to become the
gift it was meant to be.

6/17/97

It is awaiting all those who seek it.
It is there for everyone.
It is achievable, if only they try...
Heaven!

6/17/97

Pray for a blessing for each person you meet.
Pray for a gift for each one you see.
Pray for salvation for all.

(*Sirach 12:26*—To repay man according to his
deeds.)

6/17/97

In the presence of love, grow.
In the presence of God, be humble.
In the Presence that is the Eucharist.

(*Habakkuk 1:5*—And be utterly amazed.)

6/23/97

Sin covers many hearts.
Confession cleanses them.

(*Haggai 1:7*—Consider your ways.)

6/23/97

To speak truthfully with kindness, does not hurt.
To speak truthfully but with venom is a sin, and
that always hurts.

(*Psalms 147:21*—May my mouth speak the praise of
the Lord.)

6/23/97

Pray for the church,
Pray for the clergy,
Pray for the world.

(*John 6:45*—They shall all be taught by God.)

6/25/97

Benediction, often forgotten by priests and by laity.
Benediction, sometimes disregarded and seen as
meaningless.
Benediction, an important grace from God, where,
in humility, people can show they adore and
love God.

6/26/97

In a bishop's hands, is the authority of the church.
In a bishop's life, should be the example of Jesus.
In a bishop's heart, must be the love of Jesus; then
he truly is a bishop.

(*Jeremiah 5:1*—If you can find a man that executeth
judgment and seeketh faith.)

6/28/97

Making your whole life a prayer, is making your life
complete.
Making your whole life Mine, is what makes life
worth living.
Making your whole life an offering to God, makes
your life a true gift.

(*Mark 8:35-36*—Anyone who loses his life for My
sake, and for the sake of the gospel, will save
it.)

6/28/97

Making hard decisions is sometimes necessary, but
if they are made in love and for the right
reasons, then you know what you do is correct.

(*Luke 9:62*—Once the hand is laid on the plough,
no one who looks back is fit for the kingdom of
God.)

7/3/97

The world is a jewel, but today it is a jewel that is
hidden in the darkness by a blanket of sin.
To remove this blanket so the jewel can shine
brightly again, the world only needs to love.

(*Isaiah 66:22*—And the new earth I shall make.)

7/8/97

Being a servant of Mine, means being loving at all
times.
Being a servant of Mine, means being forgiving at
all times.
Being a servant of Mine, means being truthful at all
times.

Without truth in your life, how can you be with Me,
for I am the truth?
Without love in your life, how can you reflect Me,
for I am love?
Without forgiveness in your life, how can you
spread My love? For, in truth, without
forgiveness, there is not love.

(*Psalms 19:9*—The command of the Lord is clear,
enlightening the eye.)

7/10/97

My Son carried the cross of sin on His shoulders, as
He walked to Calvary.
My Son carried the weight of sin on His heart, as
they hung Him high on the cross.
My Son carried the defeat of sin on His soul, as a
sign of His love for all.

Now people need to carry this truth in their hearts
to be saved.

7/10/97

Do not fear anything in life, then you can truly live.
Do not fear anything in life, by trusting in Me.
Do not fear anything in life, and then see evil
    cannot harm you.

(Isaiah 63:17—Fear you not.)

7/27/97

A man one day sat looking in a mirror.
All he could see before him was his faults: his gray
    hair, his balding, his overweight, his wrinkles,
    his aging, and his body becoming weaker.

He did not understand this was his pride saying,
    "You are no longer perfect. What a
    disappointment you are."
He forgot that many of the faults he saw were not
    faults at all, but a natural part of life.
He forgot this is what happens to all people; none
    can avoid it.
He forgot to see the good in himself and his life.

Yes, these things were happening, but they were
    happening as they should.
Now, though, this man was letting them become a
    distraction in his life.
Instead of leading a joyful life, he began to live one
    full of worry and concern over tomorrow.

Nothing changed; he still got older; his worrying
    prevented nothing, except his enjoying life as he
    should.
He died and went to the grave with his worries, and
    having wasted much of his life.
If only he had seen each moment for what it is, a
    treasure, and not worried about what was to
    come, he could have lived a joyful life as he was
    meant to.

133.

Today, so many are like this man, worrying about
   tomorrow and forgetting about today.

If you make today important in your life, tomorrow
   can be a joy.
If you make each moment one of love, tomorrow will
   be a treasure to enjoy, not a burden to suffer.
If you make now God's time, then eternity is yours
   in love.

(*Isaiah 7:9*—Unless your faith is firm, you shall not
   be firm.)
(*Matthew 12:32*—Either in this age or the age to
   come.)

7/28/97

Trust...easy to say, but hard to achieve.
Love...easy to receive, but hard to give.
Hope...easy to have, but hard to follow.

When you have hope in your life, often it is hard to
   follow the path that hope leads you down.
When you have love in your life, often it is hard to
   share that love as you should.
When you have trust in your life, often it is hard to
   keep it there when little seems to be achieved.

With true love of Jesus, your trust is strengthened
   and you never lose hope, for in Jesus you find
   your true self, the self of love.

(*Proverbs 2:2*—Inclining your heart to
   understanding.)

7/28/97

In prayer, you find Me.
In prayer, you find yourself.
In prayer, you find the truth.

(*Daniel 14:4*—The living God who made heaven and earth and has dominion over mankind.)

7/29/97

Forward in love, backward in sin,
Forward in humility, backward in pride,
Forward in faith, backward in doubt.

Go forward in Jesus, for in Him you will never step back.

7/30/97

In the love of God you live.
Outside of it you die.

(*Job 15:11*—Are the consolations of God not enough for you?)

8/1/97

The rose of love is in all men's hearts, and it will grow, if they nurture it.
The rose of love is in all men's souls, and it will give off a sweet perfume, if they care for it.
The rose of love is Jesus My Son, and with the food of the sacraments and the light of prayer, all men can let their hearts grow in His love to become roses of heaven.

(*Zechariah 2:15*—And He will dwell among you.)

135.

8/1/97

A sacrifice is a gift of love.
A sacrifice is a giving of self.
A sacrifice is a treasure of hope.

When you sacrifice for Me, it becomes a gift of your
self given to Me in the hope of finding the
eternal treasure of heaven.
A hope I will fulfill in My love.

(*Proverbs 22:1*—The Lord loves the pure of heart.)
(*Zechariah 9:8*—I have regard for their affliction.)

8/3/97

Spirituality is not a turning your back on this life;
it is an enhancing of it.
If, in your search to grow in spiritual wisdom, you
turn your back on this life, then you cannot
grow.

This life is part of your whole existence and should
be treasured as part of it, not the most
important part, but an integral part of it.

To live this life to the full in My love is why you are
here, and to ignore that, is to close your heart
to the precious gift of life I give to you.

Eternal life in heaven is the goal, but this life on
earth is the path, the path that should lead to
Jesus.

8/3/97

Friends in Christ are friends for life.

(*Ephesians 6:18*—All the holy ones.)

8/3/97

Totally God's, means totally loving.

(*Luke 1:47*—My spirit rejoices in God.)

8/4/97

In prayer, live.
In prayer, give.
In prayer, believe.

8/11/97

In baptism, you are sealed in Jesus.
In baptism, you are made Mine.
In baptism, you are filled with the Spirit.

A soul consecrated to God,
A body given in love,
A child offered eternity.

(*Jeremiah 52:20*—Made for the house of the Lord.)

8/20/97

As I look upon the earth and see all the turmoil, confusion, and sin, I see a family trying to destroy itself, I see a family that is so insecure that it would rather die than try to change and live.
Mankind is on a course of self-destruction and unless it changes its heart and mind, it will succeed in its wish.

Like any parent who loves his children, I do not want My family on earth to hurt itself, but like any parent who loves his children, I will not force My will upon them.
I offer My love, My guidance, and My caring.

How I want mankind to accept these and live, and how I want mankind to open its eyes to the reality of what it is doing to itself, and how, unless it changes, it will certainly die.

(*Ezekiel 2:4*—Hard of face and obstinate of heart are they.)

8/20/97

Put every moment in My hands and then every moment becomes worthwhile.

(*Sirach 17:3*—He endows man with a strength of His own.)

8/21/97

To evangelize, you need to be strong in the
sacraments and in prayer.
It is through these you find the truth to share, the
strength to give, and the humility to truly serve
Me.

(*Baruch 3:14*—Learn where prudence is, where
strength, where understanding.)

8/21/97

Your body is a temple for the Spirit, and so it
should be treated with respect.
Your body is a gift of My love, and so it should be
cared for.
Your body is a part of the miracle of creation, and
so it should be shown understanding of its
needs to exist in creation.

Respect your body and treat this gift of My love with
the understanding of how it was created, and
why.

(*Baruch 3:35*—Shining with joy for their maker.)

8/21/97

Prayer is a necessity in life, that is often seen as a
cross.
Prayer is a necessity in life, if you want to live as
you should.
Prayer is a necessity in life, for when it is prayer to
Me and for good, then it brings all that is
necessary in life.

(*Hosea 10:12*—For it is time to seek the Lord.)
(*Luke 11:9*—And I tell you, ask and you shall
receive.)

8/22/97

Silence sometimes can be a grace, if it prevents you from tripping over your tongue.

8/22/97

Do not worry over little frustrations.
Walk past them, or they can become big problems.

8/23/97

To wash your soul clean of sin, means bathing in the river of forgiveness offered by My Son, through the power of the Holy Spirit in the sacrament of confession.
It is here you are forgiven, and it is here you are healed and given the graces to overcome sin in your life.

8/24/97

A child's heart is within each person.
A child's love is within each heart.
A child's need for love is within the heart of each person, and if they turn to the heart of Jesus, they will find it waiting there for them.

(Isaiah 7:2—The heart of the king.)

8/25/97

In times of confusion, think of Jesus.
In times of uncertainty, think of Jesus.
In times of distress, think of Jesus.
In Jesus, find peace and comfort, and in Jesus find
   Me.

(*Ephesians 4:21*—As truth is in Jesus.)

8/25/97

In a marriage there will be difficult moments, but it
   is in these moments you show how strong is
   your love.

(*Jonah 2:3*—Out of my distress, I called to the
   Lord.)

8/25/97

With the Eucharist as the center of your life, life
   becomes a celebration of love, life becomes a
   joy, and life becomes what it is supposed to
   be...holy.

(*Ezekiel 20:12*—The Lord Who made them holy.)

8/26/97

The joy of love is a joy all should have, for all are
   loved.
It is just that some do not know it.

(*John 8:42*—You would love me.)

141.

8/27/97

Imagine a world filled with love, a world where there
is no hate, no anger, and no sin.
When you imagine this, you imagine how the world
first was when I created it, and you imagine
how it will be again, when I welcome mankind
back into My arms.

8/28/97

In Mary's arms, all can find true love, for it is in
her arms that she will bring you closer to My
Son Jesus.

(*Acts 9:41*—He gave her His hand.)

8/28/97

Reunion of hearts begins when you return to Jesus.

(*Psalms 103:10*—He has not dealt with us as our
sins merit.)

8/30/97

See in money a way to help others, not yourself;
then money becomes a gift of love, a gift to be
shared.

(*Isaiah 30:29*—And be merry of heart.)

9/4/97

When My Son offers you His love, all He asks in
 return is your love.
When My Son offers you His heart, all He asks in
 return is your heart.
When My Son offers you His life, all He asks in
 return is your life.

What He offers is a love-filled life in His heart, and
 all you need to do is return to Him.

(*Proverbs 3:5*—Trust in the Lord with all your
 heart.)

9/4/97

May your heart reflect My love,
May your life reflect My love,
May your soul reflect My love,
And may you live with Me eternally in heaven.

(*Jeremiah 44:25*—Keep your vows; carry out your
 resolutions.)

143.

9/5/97

When My Son comes, He comes in love and in
    forgiveness, so why are many frightened of what
    lies ahead?
If they have lived a good and holy life, they have
    nothing to fear.

These feelings of fear are there for many because
    they are not living as they should...living for
    God.
These feelings are their consciences saying, "Look
    at yourself and change your heart to be one of
    love, not of self, not of power, not judgmental,
    not condemning of others, not of excuses to sin,
    and not of despair over others, when you need
    to change yourself."
These feelings are your conscience saying, "First
    change yourself, then you can help others to
    change, for if you are not living how you should,
    what sort of an example will you be to those
    who need to be brought back to Jesus?"

(*Job 15:22*—He despairs of escaping the darkness,
    and looks ever for the sword.)

9/9/97

For physical ailments, see a physician,
For spiritual ailments, a priest...for each is a gift
    from Me to you.

(Matthew 4:23—Curing every disease and illness
    among the people.)
(Ecclesiasticus 3:13—His labor is a gift from God.)
(2 Maccabees 15:8—Mindful of the help they had
    received from heaven.)

9/9/97

Prayer, a gift of love.
Prayer, a grace of love.
Prayer, a sign of love.
To those who believe.

(*Ecclesiasticus 3:8*—A time to love.)

9/11/97

Impress upon your heart the need to love others,
    for it is in loving others you show your love for
    Me.

(*Sirach 39:26*—Chief of all needs for human life.)

9/11/97

Show more consideration of others, just as you
    would expect them to consider you.

(*Psalms 107:31*—Such kindness.)

9/11/97

In your thoughts of others, think only of goodness,
    of helping, and of loving; then you think as you
    should.

(*Wisdom 11:5*—They in their need were benefited.)

9/11/97

The gifted are those who give, not receive.

(*Psalms 34:10*—You holy ones.)

145.

To see from the soul, you need to release your spirit
    into My love.
To see from the heart, you need to fill your heart
    with My love.
To see in love, fill your heart and soul with My
    Spirit by sacraments, by prayer, and by
    complete acceptance of My will.

(*Wisdom 12:1*—Imperishable spirit.)

9/17/97

The whole of heaven looks down to earth and offers
    love, and offers help to love.
All the angels and saints long to bring souls back to
    Me and home, to share in My glorious love
    eternally.
Heaven awaits those who will listen to its call, a call
    to God and a call to peace in eternity.

Mankind is being offered all it needs to find its true
    self and its true home.
All it has to do is listen and heed My call.

(*Matthew 26:35*—I will not deny you.)

9/17/97

If you pray for guidance, you must listen for the
    answer.

9/23/97

Try never to fear...trust.
Try never to worry...believe.
Try never to doubt...have faith,
Then all is possible.

(*Isaiah 10:20*—Lean upon the Lord.)

9/30/97

A heart of love,
A heart of caring,
A heart of sharing,
This is what the heart of mankind should be.

(*Jeremiah 9:23*—Bring about kindness.)

9/30/97

In My name, you serve.
For My glory, you work.
With My praises, you speak.
Always for Me is what brings true humility.

(*Zechariah 9:11*—Your covenant with Me.)

9/30/97

If you open your mouth in love, I am there.
If you open your heart in love, I am there.
If you open your soul in love, I am there.
In love, I am always there.

147.

10/4/97

Rejoice in My love.
Rejoice in your life.
Rejoice in My love in your life.

(*Daniel 12:3*—Shine brightly.)

10/4/97

All men are brothers.
All women are sisters.
All of mankind is family.

When they understand this, and live as a family,
    paradise will return to earth.

(*Isaiah 2:17*—And the Lord alone will be exalted on
    that day.)

10/10/97

Reflections of love,
Reflections of grace,
Reflections of My Son is how mankind can be,
    if they trust and believe in Me.

(*Wisdom 11:26*—Lord and Lover of souls.)

10/10/97

Submerge your soul in the sacraments, and find
    your soul delighted.

10/10/97

Poverty abounds, and so does greed.
Poverty ignored, is greed appeased.
Poverty for some, means plenty for others.

A large sin upon the world is the poverty that is
    forced upon many, so that the greedy can
    appease their insatiable appetites.
A sin that will bring many to account on their final
    day.

(*Psalms 146:4*—When they breathe their last, they
    return to the earth.)

10/11/97

Be aware of the needs of others, and respond to
    them in love.
Be aware of the pains of others, and respond to
    them in love.
Be aware of the loneliness of others, and respond to
    them in love.
Become love to all in all situations, and find you
    become a welcome breath from Me to all.

(*Isaiah 6:10*—Their heart understands.)

10/13/97

Mankind lost in itself, needs to look beyond self and
    see the love in creation that is My gift to all.
Mankind lost in itself, needs to look beyond self and
    see what awaits those who love and those who
    sin.
Mankind lost in itself, needs to look beyond self and
    see how it needs to change, if it wants the
    eternal reward of heaven.

(*Job 15:17*—I will show you, if you listen to Me.)

149.

10/14/97

A Holy Land awaits to be flooded with the love the
   peace flight brings.
A Holy Land awaits you holy people.
A Holy Land awaits the prayers and the sacrifices
   the peace flight brings in the love of God, as an
   example on how to be holy.

(*Isaiah 23:1*—The news reaches them.)

10/14/97

Israel, land of hope, land of the prophets, land of
   God.
Israel, land of confusion, land of hate, land of
   sadness.
Israel, land that felt the touch of Jesus' feet, Jesus'
   love, and Jesus' blood.

A land where the victory was won, and yet still the
   battle rages, because men do not accept the
   truth.
When the truth is embraced in this land, the hope
   of the future will be found, and Jesus will be
   proclaimed as Lord.

(*Psalms 40:4*—Many shall look on in awe, and they
   shall trust in the Lord.)

10/16/97

I love each person in a way they could never
  imagine.
The love I have for mankind is the true love of God
  which always forgives, always understands,
  always comforts and cares for, always gives,
  always wants the best for, and always is there.

My love is an example for mankind, and in the life
  of My Son Jesus, that love is shown plainly in
  the hope that all will try to live as He did.
I love My children and I want only their love in
  return, so that together we can celebrate
  eternal life.

(*John 6:45*—They shall all be taught by God.)

10/18/97

If you praise yourself, you become full of pride and
  empty of Me.
If you praise Me, you become full of humility and
  empty of self.
If you praise Me, do it from your heart and find
  your thoughts of self disappear.

10/18/97

My Son's love grows in each person by the grace of
  the sacrifices they make.
It is in the giving you grow.
It is in the sacrifices you are rewarded, and it is in
  the difficult moments you are graced.

Jesus says to all who follow Him that sacrifices are
  needed, but live by His example and see them
  as welcome crosses used to save souls.

(*Jeremiah 46:18*—As I live, says the King.)

151.

10/18/97

In the pursuit of heaven, you will find love is the
path you must walk if you wish to succeed, for
heaven is love, only love.

(*Ephesians 6:16*—In all circumstances.)

10/21/97

Mary, an example of love.
Mary, an example of sacrifice.
Mary, an example of silence.

In her love of God, Mary kept silent as she saw her
Son sacrificed.
This is an example for all those who sacrifice.

10/21/97

The mother of God became the mother of mankind
when she bore My Son, Who is brother to all.

(*1 Corinthians 15:23*—Those who belong to Christ.)

10/21/97

The Holy Family,
The family of God.
The Holy Family,
How all families can be.

(*Micah 3:11*—The Lord in the midst of us.)

10/23/97

Make each day, a day full of love.
Make each day, a day that is a prayer.
Make each day, a day you offer to Me, then you
truly live each day.

(*Luke 1:47*—My spirit rejoices in God.)

10/23/97

Receive others, as you expect to be received.
Listen to others, as you expect to be listened to.
Respect others, as you expect to be respected.

For all are equal in My eyes, and they should be in
yours also.

(*Colossians 3:14*—And over all these, put on love;
that is the bond of perfection.)

10/23/97

To reflect My love, offer love to all.
To reflect My caring, care for all.
To reflect My truth, be truthful to all.

I am the truth, and if you want others to know My
love, be truthful in your caring for them and
show them by your example, that you are My
servant of love.

(*Acts 10:34*—In truth, I see that God shows no
partiality.)

10/23/97

Love equals life, as sin equals death.
If you want to live in eternal love, you must live this
    life in love.
If you want to find only eternal death, then
    continue to sin, and you will find what you
    seek.

Love in My name, and live.
Live in My name, and love eternally.

10/23/97

In My mercy, all can be forgiven.
In My grace, all can come to heaven.
In My heart, all can reside, if only they want to.

(*Malachi 3:17*—And I will have compassion on
    them.)

10/27/97

When you see a bird flying in the sky or a plant
    growing in the ground,
When you see the sun shining brightly or the moon
    high above,
When you see each person in every country or you
    see a family at home,

See the beauty of My creation, and see My love.

11/8/97

When a child ignores his parents' wishes, he hurts the parents.
When a child sins and listens to no advice, he hurts the parents.
When a child lives in a way that leads deeper and deeper into sin, ignoring all the good advice of his parents, then the parents are truly hurt, but it is a hurt that can be lifted when the child returns to the way of good.

If parents pray for their children and offer them to Me through My Son Jesus, then My Holy Spirit will touch the children, and My daughter Mary will be there helping them to accept that touch.

(*Revelation 2:13*—Hold fast to My Name.)
(*Sirach 44:20*—When tested.)

11/8/97

As your Father, I love you.
As your God, I created you.
As your destiny, I welcome you.

When people accept Me as their God, Who created them in love and call Me Father from their heart, then people will find their destiny is an eternity of love in My heavenly home.

(*Psalms 42:5*—The house of God.)

11/8/97

Be aware of Jesus in your life by receiving Him in the Eucharist each day, for in the Eucharist I give you your daily bread.

(*Ephesians 5:32*—This is a great mystery.)

155.

11/11/97

There is a constant war between good and evil
   which will never end until My Son Jesus comes
   and claims the souls which are His, and
   condemns those who are not, into the abyss of
   hell.

(*Psalms 125:5*—May the Lord send down with the
   wicked.)

11/18/97

The bread of life...Jesus.
The wine of salvation...Jesus.
The Son of God...Jesus.

There is no other who is One with Me and My Holy
   Spirit, and there is no other way to heaven
   except through Jesus.

(*Wisdom 12:13*—Neither is there any God besides.)

11/18/97

To accept sin or to close your eyes to it for any
   reason, is a sin itself.
If you do not stand against sin, then you must be
   for it, as there is no in-between.

(*Wisdom 12:2*—Warn them and remind them of the
   sins they are committing.)

11/20/97

My Son opened His arms on the cross to reach out in an embrace of love for the whole world, an embrace that brings eternal joy to those who walk into His arms and say yes to His offer of salvation.

(*1 Corinthians 15:54*—Death is swallowed up in victory.)

11/20/97

My Son prepared Himself for His trial with prayer. If Jesus, Who is the Son of God, did this, then He clearly showed this is what all mankind must do when facing trial or tribulation.

Today, prayer is needed more than ever, for today sin spreads its web over the whole world, bringing tribulation to all.

Pray for the grace and the strength to overcome sin through My Son, and you will find that His mother Mary will be by your side, joining in your prayers, and that Jesus, My Son, will answer your call.

(*Jude 21*—Keep yourselves in the love of God, and wait for the mercy of our Lord Jesus Christ that leads to eternal life.)

157.

11/23/97

In the Eucharist, you will find all you need to come
closer to Me.
In the Eucharist, you will find all you need to live
your life in My love.
In the Eucharist, you will find My Son waiting to
answer your needs in bringing you closer to Me,
so that you can be complete in My love, My Son
Jesus.

(*Psalms 63:12*—Rejoice in God.)

11/24/97

Impatience, irritability, intolerance, and
inconsideration all come in pride and in sin.

(*Hebrews 11:13*—All these died in faith.)

11/26/97

Never believe you are alone, for you are not.
Never believe there is nothing after death, for there
is.
Never believe you are not loved, for you are.
Without these beliefs life is empty, and without
these beliefs there is no hope.

(*Luke 1:45*—Blessed are you who believed.)

11/26/97

I offer to all people love and forgiveness, and the
chance to become anew in Me.
I offer to all people My hand to hold, as they walk
through life.
I offer to all people an eternity with Me, of love in
heaven.

I am there for all people; none will be turned away,
and none will be refused My eternal love in
heaven, if they ask in truth and in repentance.

(*Acts 2:21*—And it shall be that everyone shall be
saved who calls on the name of the Lord.)

11/30/97

A man must live in love, or else he truly is not a
man.

(*Sirach 3:1*—Do so, that you may live.)

12/7/97

In prayer you talk to Me.
In prayer you open your heart to Me.
In prayer you find a way closer to Me.

If you want to come closer to Me and open your
heart to My love, talk to Me in prayer.

(*Matthew 6:9*—Our Father in heaven.)

159.

12/9/97

When you think the Holy Spirit is not working,
   He is.
When you think you have failed, the Holy Spirit
   succeeds.
When you think it is not possible, the Holy Spirit
   makes it possible.
When you work in the Holy Spirit, know that
   anything is possible, and if you trust in Him
   you will succeed.

(*1 Corinthians 15:58*—Be firm, steadfast, always
   fully devoted to the work of the Lord, knowing
   that in the Lord your labor is not in vain.)

12/9/97

The feelings of others are always needed to be kept
   in mind, otherwise you may unwittingly hurt
   them.

(*Ecclesiasticus 5:1*—Be not hasty in your utterance.)

12/9/97

Making peace with others is important, for without
   peace how can there be love?

(*Joshua 22:27*—Peace offerings.)

12/9/97

Prayer and the sacraments combined, make the
   path to Me clearer and the walk spirit-filled.

(*Psalms 142:4*—My Spirit.)
(*Lamentations 5:2*—In full measures.)
(*Luke 18:1*—Pray always without becoming weary.)

12/12/97

The key to life is love, and the key to love is Jesus,
Who opens all hearts and offers all true life.

12/14/97

My Son Jesus came to the world to forgive, to love,
and to lead home to heaven My children.
These are the messages He brought, and those who
follow Him must bring the same messages to the
world.
He did not come to condemn the world but to save
it, and He explained to all who would listen that
it was their own actions that would condemn
them, unless they truly repented.

Jesus never said that people who sought His
love with a true heart would be condemned,
even if they did make mistakes. Jesus said they
would be forgiven.
Jesus never said that people who sought His love
with a true heart would be denied. Jesus said
they would be loved.
Jesus never said that people who sought His love
with a true heart would be sent to hell. He said
heaven was theirs.

The message of Jesus was and is love, not
condemnation.

Yet today many can see only punishment and
suffering to come in His words. They have
forgotten His love.

Today many look for the end times instead of
looking to His love.
Today many look for the evil to come, and are quick
to accuse and condemn, instead of offering His
love.

161.

Today many claim knowledge of the "end times,"
  when Jesus, Himself, said no one knows the
  time or place, except Me, His Father.
Today many forget His words, not to worry about
  tomorrow, for that will take care of itself.
Today so many are trapped in thoughts of wars,
  disasters, and tragedies to come, they forget
  about the tragedy of today, with so many souls
  away from Me.

They do not see the war that rages every day; the
  war of good against evil, and they do not see
  how, if they are not part of that war by receiving
  the sacraments, praying, and taking the
  message of Jesus to the world, the result will be
  disastrous for many.

Today souls need to be saved, and if people try to
  help in this, then tomorrow will be a joy.

(*Ephesians 5:15*—Watch carefully then how you
  live, not as foolish persons but as wise.)

12/14/97

Prayers of love, are answered in love.
Prayers of joy, are answered in joy.
Prayers of hope, are answered in hope.
Pray in love, and have the joy of knowing your
  hopes will be fulfilled.

(*Psalms 118:15*—The joyful shout of deliverance.)

12/14/97

Be a lamb in a world of wolves.
Be a light in a world of darkness.
Be a servant in a world of pride...

Then you are as Jesus showed you how to be.
You are a servant of love.

(*Ezekiel 3:9*—Fear them not.)

12/21/97

Being kind to others is nothing extraordinary, for
this is how mankind was created to be, and it is
each person's way to live, if they wish to be
what they were created for.

12/28/97

Through all opposition, walk in love.
Through all hatred, show only love.
Through all the attempts to stop you, offer only the
defense of love.

Then, in love, victory will be yours as you show the
strength I give you in My Son Jesus' name, and
by the power of My Holy Spirit.

(*Psalms 145:2*—Every day I will bless you.)

163.

12/29/97

Prayer...spiritual communication, when it is from
  the heart.
Prayer..spiritually strengthening, when it is from
  the soul.
Prayer...spiritually enlightening, when it is from a
  humble longing to love Me more.

(*Romans 12:1*—Your spiritual worship.)

12/29/97

In the Eucharist place your soul, and then in your
  soul, find peace.

(*1 John 3:24*—From the spirit that He gave us.)

12/30/97

Make your life a prayer by making all you do a
  prayer.

(*Sirach 36:17*—The prayer of the lowly pierces the
  clouds; it does not rest till it reaches its goal.)

12/30/97

A happy heart brings joy to others. Always be happy
  in Jesus, and see His joy touch others.

(*Luke 1:19*—This good news.)

1/2/98

Your Father,
Everyone's Father.

Your God,
Everyone's God.

Your eternity,
Everyone's eternity.

This is what I am, I should be, and I offer to all.

1/2/98

Pray for the grace to be able to express your love in
each word of every prayer.

(*James 1:2*—Consider it all joy.)

1/2/98

History means little, unless you learn from it.

1/4/98

Focusing on the Eucharist, brings clarity to your
work.
Focusing on the Eucharist, keeps Jesus in your life.
Focusing on the Eucharist, reminds you of the love
Jesus has for you.

(*Jeremiah 31:35*—Whose name is the Lord of Hosts.)
(*Psalms 24:5*—Their saving God.)

165.

1/4/98

The answer to your prayers is Jesus—never forget
   that.

(Deuteronomy 7:13—He will love, and bless, and
   multiply you.)

1/6/98

When you look to blame others for problems in your
   life, you often forget to look at yourself and see
   where you went wrong.

(Esther 5:25—No one but you.)

1/9/98

The road to heaven is narrow, but My Son's heart is
   wide.

(Tobit 8:17—With happiness and mercy.)

1/9/98

Do not fear death.
Remember, I wait for you.

(Sirach 7:32—That your blessing may be complete.)

Be a friend to the lonely,
Be a help to the needy,
Be a gift to the poor.

Make your life one of friendship to all those in
    need, and find by helping the poor, your life
    becomes a gift that brings love to even the
    loneliest.

(*Job 13:8*—Advocate on behalf of God.)

You must try to pray in every way possible.
In all you do, in all you say, in all you think, and in
    all your love.
Pray, pray, pray, for so many today do not say even
    one prayer, therefore you should carry their
    burden by praying more.
This then becomes a sacrifice of love, and the more
    you do this, think of this, and say this, the
    more you love and the more you grow closer to
    God.

(*Isaiah 45:7*—Do all these things.)

If it were not a sacrifice to do My work, then it
    would not be a giving of self and an offering of
    love.

(*Romans 8:37*—In all these things we conquer
    overwhelmingly, through Him Who loved us.)

167.

<u>1/20/98</u>

When you see others in distress, show compassion.
When you see others in need, give.
When you see others in weakness, bring them My
    strength.

(*Isaiah 15:5*—They utter rending cries.)

<u>1/20/98</u>

When you appreciate the love that is in your
    marriage, then the marriage grows.
When you ignore it, then the marriage can die.

(*Sirach 40:26*—He who has it, need seek no other
    support.)

<u>1/21/98</u>

Many have sorrow on their heart.
Many have pain within.
Many have souls that are scarred.

All can be healed in My Son, if only they want to be,
    and if only they ask.

(*2 Chronicles 26:5*—Prepared seek God.)

<u>1/21/98</u>

Be aware of others' feelings, needs, and desires;
    then see how they are the same as yours, and
    see that their answers, just like yours, are in
    Me.

(*Psalms 72:13*—He shows pity to the needy and the
    poor.)

1/21/98

Be as a child, then you be as you should.

(*Luke 16:8*—Children of the light.)

1/24/98

Focus on prayer,
Focus on the sacraments,
Focus on obedience,

Then be strong in Me.

(*Proverbs 1:33*—He who obeys me dwells in
security.)

2/6/98

Place all your life into My service, and you will find
joy and peace in eternity.

(*Ezekiel 2:8*—I shall give you.)

2/6/98

Make all your life Mine,
Make all your life love of Me,
Make all your life service for Me,
And find I will be with you forever.

(*Sirach 4:28*—Even to the death, fight for truth, and
the Lord your God will battle for you.)

169.

7/2/98

A sharing heart is a heart of love.

(*Isaiah 58:7*—Sharing your bread with the hungry.)

2/8/98

Never take advantage of another, for if you do it is a sin of self, of greed, and of not caring for another.

(*2 Maccabees 5:7*—He did not gain.)

2/8/98

To touch hearts, pray.
To touch souls, pray.
To touch the lost, pray.

Pray that God gives you the graces to do so.

(*Isaiah 48:1*—And invoke the God of Israel.)

2/8/98

Never ignore a call for help.
Never turn away from someone in need.
Never be afraid to help those in need, and never turn away in fear from those who call to you, for if you do, you turn from Jesus.

(*Sirach 28:7*—Think of the commandments.)

2/10/98

It is a wise man who holds his tongue in times of
uncertainty.
It is a wise man who remains quiet rather than
criticize another.
It is a wise man who shows discretion in his
remarks about others.

(*Ezekiel 16:5*—With pity and compassion.)

2/10/98

It is good to give with a willing heart, but it is sad
to give with a begrudging heart.

2/10/98

When you give, do it in love, not for reward.

(*Job 7:2*—He is a slave who longs for the shade. A
hireling who waits for his wages.)

2/14/98

To give in love, is true giving.
To give without seeking reward, is true love.
To give for God, is true life.

(*Sirach 2:1*—When you come to serve the Lord.)

171.

2/14/98

With each moment, love.
With each breath, love.
With each action, love. Then you live.

(*Ecclesiasticus 3:8*—A time to love.)

3/31/98

In the presence of My Son Jesus, you come into the
 presence of Me.
In the grace of the Holy Spirit, you come into the
 grace of Me.
In the grace I give when you are in My presence,
 you also are in the presence of My Son Jesus,
 and My Holy Spirit, Who are One with Me.

(*Romans 11:36*—For from Him and through Him and
 for Him, are all things.)

4/7/98

My family throughout the earth lives uncertain in
 the future.
This is because they do not trust completely in Me.
If they did, there would only be certainty.

(*Sirach 39:33*—Every need when it comes He fills.)

4/7/98

Blessed are they who serve God,
Blessed are they who love God,
Blessed are they who believe in God,
And all are called to be blessed.

(*John 12:13*—Blessed is he who comes in the name
 of the Lord.)

4/9/98

Christianity, the cradle of love,
Christianity, the house of hope,
Christianity, the truth of truths,
And all found in the universal church of love, that
    brings hope to all by living in the truth.

(*Luke 2:75*—In holiness and righteousness.)

4/10/98 (Good Friday)

You feel an internal distress, a spiritual one.
You feel an internal emptiness, a love-suffering one.
You feel an internal draining, a friendship one.

As a friend of Jesus, you feel distressed as your
    spirit cries out to your suffering Lord, Whom
    you love so much, and with the realization of
    how He suffered for you, comes an emptiness
    that will only be filled on Easter day.

(*Romans 1:16*—It is the power of God for the
salvation of everyone.)

4/10/98

Throughout eternity, this day reverberates with the
    love of God for man.
Throughout eternity, this day shines forth the light
    of God's forgiveness.
Throughout eternity, this day overcomes all sin and
    suffering, for this day is the day My Son Jesus
    shed His blood to wash away the sins of
    mankind.

(*Luke 1:50*—His mercy is from age to age.)

4/10/98

Under the cross is a shadow of love and forgiveness.
Under the cross is a shadow of peace and
    contentment.
Under the cross is a shadow of protection and
    security.
Stand in it, and find all this waiting for you.

(*Jeremiah 17:19*—My fortress, my refuge, in the day
    of distress.)

4/13/98

The world was created to be a paradise, but man in
    his freedom tries to destroy this gift.
The world was given to mankind as a gift that man
    should cherish and care for.
The world was created as a beautiful gift of My love
    for mankind.

Why does mankind forget or ignore this, and does
    its best to destroy what I have given it?

Love the planet, love the plants, love the animals,
    and most important of all, love Me and each
    other; then find paradise once more in your
    world.

(*Sirach 3:1*—Do so, that you may live.)

4/13/98

A friendly heart, is a heart of love.
A loving heart, is a heart of giving.
A giving heart, is a heart of service,

And this is the heart I love to give all it needs to
serve Me.

(*Jeremiah 9:23*—For with such I am pleased.)

4/14/98

A man who has faith in Me can achieve anything,
for his faith will be the power of God in his soul,
and by My power, anything is possible.

(*Proverbs 4:26*—And let all your ways be sure.)

4/14/98

On a throne of love, I sit watching the world turn.
On a throne of love, I sit offering that love to all.
On a throne of love, I sit waiting for the world to
turn back to Me and accept what I offer.

(*Isaiah 9:6*—His dominion is vast and forever
peaceful.)

175.

4/30/98

There are many called to do My work and to spread
   My love.
The people who accept the call, at times carry a
   heavy burden, because there are many more
   who refuse to accept their call.
It is by the service of those who answer the call that
   My love will be shared amongst mankind, and it
   is by their service that evil will be overcome in
   many hearts.

Those who do not respond to My call will one day
   come to know what they have refused, and will
   be filled with sadness that they did not listen.
They will come to understand that by their denial,
   others had to carry much more, and that by
   their denial, suffering remained on earth longer
   than it should have.

On this day, when the truth is shown to those who
   walked away from My call, there will be many
   broken hearts, and many asking, "Why was I so
   foolish?"

(Psalms 106:6—We have done wrong and are guilty.)
(Isaiah 52:15—So shall He startle many.)

4/30/98

Insecurity breeds fear, and fear so often can lead to
   sin.
Be secure in Me, and be strengthened against sin.

(Hebrews 12:12—So strengthen your drooping
   hands and your weakness.)

5/2/98

United in prayer,
United in the sacraments,
United in Jesus,
The church will grow.

5/2/98

A humble man never proclaims his humility, for he
never believes he has it.

5/5/98

In My mercy, all can be saved,
In My mercy, all can be forgiven,
In My mercy, all can be brought to heaven.

My mercy is Jesus, Whose divine love is waiting to
forgive all, so they can be saved and brought to
heaven.

(*Titus 3:5*—Because of His mercy.)

5/6/98

Love is like a flower, it grows in the light but will
die in the darkness.

(*John 12:36*—Believe in the light.)

5/6/98

Life is a gift, so live each day as an appreciation of
what you are given.

(*Psalms 51:10*—Let me hear sounds of joy and
gladness.)

177.

5/15/98

When you make the effort to love Me, you are
   rewarded.

(*Psalms 19:12*—Brings much reward.)

5/15/98

To make your life Mine, means to make the choice
   that leads to eternal bliss.

(*Proverbs 2:19*—Gain the paths of life.)

5/15/98

Show kindness always, and then show your true
   self.

(*Daniel 12:3*—Shine brightly.)

5/19/98

With an open heart all is possible, but with a closed
   heart much is impossible.

(*John 12:40*—Understand with their heart.)
(*Isaiah 40:31*—They that hope in the Lord will
   renew their strength; they will soar as with
   eagles' wings.)

5/19/98

To share, to love, and to be happy...doing so are
   gifts that bring joy to all.

(*1 Timothy 4:14*—Do not neglect the gift you have.)

5/28/98

In a day, you can live in love or you can live in self.
Living in love, the day is a joy where you care for
   everyone and everything.
Living in self, the day is a burden where only your
   needs are before you and often weigh heavily
   upon you.

(*Job 10:22*—Where darkness is the only light.)

6/6/98

A title means little, unless there is love in the
   heart.

(*Philippians 2:8*—He humbled himself.)

6/7/98

As an offering of love, your life becomes filled with
   the Holy Trinity.
You are filled with your Father's love, you are filled
   with My Son's mercy, and you are filled with My
   Spirit's gifts and graces.
Your life has become a Trinitarian one, and it could
   be no other way, if you truly offer yourself to Me
   in love.

6/9/98

The truth is the foundation you must always stand
   on, for the truth is Jesus, and from Jesus
   comes all truth.

(*Proverbs 8:7*—Yes, the truth.)
(*Job 21:9*—Of God.)

179.

Joy of joys,
Love of loves,
Hope of hopes,
Jesus, My Son, who brings joy into the lives of
those who hope in His love.

(*Jeremiah 17:7*—Whose hope is the Lord.)

6/10/98

Being in love with Me, means loving all of My
creations.
If you do not love what I have made in My love, how
can you love Me?

(*Sirach 1:8*—All his works.)

6/12/98

A man who trusts in God is never forsaken.

(*Matthew 21:22*—Whatever you ask for in prayer
with faith, you will receive.)

6/12/98

Ask, and you will receive,
Believe, and you will be graced,
Trust, and you will be answered.

(*Lamentations 3:25*—Good is the Lord, to one who
waits for Him.)

6/12/98

Gluttony is a sin, and those who overeat, while
others starve, should remember this.

(*Job 20:15*—God shall compel his belly to disown
them.)

6/12/98

With love in the heart, life becomes a joy.
With love in the heart, everyone becomes a brother
or a sister.
With love in the heart, you truly live seeing the joy
in each moment and the wonder in each person.

(*1 Corinthians 15:58*—The work of the Lord.)

6/16/98

It is through the sacraments that mankind can
come closer to Me, for each sacrament is filled
with graces and gifts to open hearts to Me, and
to fill lives with My love.
The sacraments are spirit-filled gifts given in the
love of My Son Jesus, so that all can be filled
with My graces.

(*2 Chronicles 6:6*—Instruments of the Lord.)

6/16/98

Be at peace in Me,
Be secure in Me,
Be strengthened in Me in the sacraments.

(*Matthew 6:11*—Our daily bread.)

181.

6/19/98

It is wise never to criticize.
It is best never to show unrest.
It is better never to criticize another, or to show
    unrest at little errors others make.

The best thing to do is to pray for them, and
    encourage them in love to see the truth.

(*Psalms 53:3*—One is wise.)
(*Psalms 108:16*—To show kindness.)

6/19/98

If you were to climb a ladder that had many of its
    steps missing, you would find it very hard, if
    not impossible to get to the top.
It is the same with the climb to heaven; if prayers
    and the sacraments are missing, it will be
    harder to reach the top, and you may even find
    you fall from the climb into the pit.

(*Jonah 2:3*—The nether world.)

6/19/98

It does not matter what the reason.
It does not matter how you can justify it.
It does not matter if no one else believes it is wrong.
A sin is always a sin, and it should be avoided at all
    costs.

(*Psalms 148:8*—The Lord loves the righteous.)
(*Psalms 148:9*—But thwarts the way of the wicked.)
(*Matthew 24:45*—Who then is the faithful and
    prudent servant.)

6/19/98

Today, many so-called prophets and visionaries
    proclaim what is contrary to the Gospel, even
    at times saying the opposite of what My Son
    Jesus said.
Yet many of the faithful listen to their words and
    see no wrong in them, even spreading the
    messages they hear.
Anything that conflicts with the Gospel is wrong.
Anything that is contradictory to what My Son
    Jesus said is wrong, and anything that is said
    against the truth is only deceit and comes from
    the evil one.

Today, many need to open their eyes to the truth
    once more and stop accepting falsehoods, for
    today, even some of the faithful spread heresy.

(*Philippians 1:15*—Some preach Christ from envy
    and rivalry.)
(*Philippians 1:17*—Proclaim Christ out of selfish
    ambition, not from pure motives.)

6/22/98

Your prayers are always heard.
Your prayers are always placed into My heart.
Your prayers are always answered in the best way.

(*Job 9:16*—If I appealed to Him, He answered my
    call.)

6/22/98

In the Rosary are many graces,
In the Rosary are many gifts,
In the Rosary are many ways of seeing God's love.

(*Isaiah 56:2*—Happy is the man who does this.)

183.

6/22/98

As My word spreads, so does love.
As My love spreads, so does true life.
As My gift of true life spreads, so does peace.

My Word is Jesus, and when His love is spread,
    peace will come into the lives of all who hear it.

(*Psalms 103:6*—The Lord does righteous deeds,
    brings justice to all the oppressed.)

6/22/98

I bring goodness,
I bring love,
I bring peace,
For that is what I AM.

(*Sirach 3:9*—A Father's blessing.)

6/29/98

Each day a gift,
Each day to be enjoyed,
Each day to be shared in love,
Then you truly live each day in the joy the gift was
    given...the gift of love.

(*Psalms 19:3*—One day to the next conveys that
    message.)

6/29/98

Accept what is put upon you with love, for that is
    what My Son Jesus did.

(*Baruch 3:37*—His beloved son.)

My mercy is shown by My Son's sacrifice on the
    cross, for it is by this act that My mercy flowed
    out to all sinners with the offer of forgiveness.

(*2 Maccabees 2:18*—He will soon have mercy on us.)

6/29/98

It is better to keep a secure heart than a secure
    bank account.

(*Psalms 73:5*—Free of the burdens of life.)

7/5/98

Justice can only be served if love is brought into all
    decisions, and kept as the focus of all
    judgments.

(*Proverbs 8:12*—Judicious knowledge.)

7/5/98

Be careful not to see only the bad in people, for
    there is good in all people.

(*1 Corinthians 7:5*—So that Satan may not tempt
    you with your lack of self-control.)

7/7/98

Never think yourself above others,
Place yourself below them, and in My love serve
    them.

(*Ephesians 5:2*—As a sacrificial offering to God.)

7/8/98

Be fair-minded to all, for that is how you would
want them to be to you.

7/8/98

In prayer, you will find peace.
In peace, you will find love.
In love, you will find Me.

7/10/98

To friends, show love.
To family, show kindness.
To all mankind, show love and kindness, making
them all your friends, for they are your family.

7/12/98

Any messages I give to the world will be those that
strengthen and support the truths of the
Catholic faith, otherwise they are not My
messages.

(*Jeremiah 16:19*—Mere frauds.)

7/12/98

If you are to serve Me, it must always be done in
truth and in love; otherwise you only serve
yourself.

(*Isaiah 30:21*—This is the way; walk in it.)

7/20/98

To remember loved ones is important.
Make all mankind your loved ones, and remember
them in all you do.

(*Obadiah 15*—All the nations.)

7/20/98

When you are confused, pray and wait for clarity.

(*Psalms 18:31*—A shield for all who trust.)

7/20/98

There are many saints in heaven, and by the grace
of My love, there will be many more.

(*Psalms 18:26*—The faithful.)

7/29/98

To those who do My work in humility, I give all they
need.
To those who do My work in pride, I give little, for
they believe they have what they need already.

(*Jeremiah 17:10*—To reward everyone according to
his ways.)

187.

7/30/98

A deeper spirituality comes from prayer, the
   sacraments, and the realization that without
   God's love in your life, there is an emptiness
   that cannot be filled.

(*Jude 19*—They live on the natural plane devoid of
   the spirit.)

7/30/98

Honest in words, in thoughts, and in actions, is the
   only way to be, if you want to serve Me.

(*Sirach 40:21*—A voice that is true.)

7/30/98

Each breath is a gift,
Each heartbeat is a gift,
Each moment of your life is a gift;
Use them wisely.

(*Ephesians 6:18*—Pray at every opportunity.)

8/1/98

Each prayer you say,
Each sacrament you receive,
Each sacrifice you make,
Brings you a step closer to Me.

(*Lamentations 3:25*—The soul that seeks Him.)

8/1/98

As My Son Jesus suffered on the cross, I suffered
with Him.
As My Son Jesus' heart was filled with pain from
the sins of mankind, I shared in that pain.
As My Son Jesus took His last breath and cried
from His soul to mankind, "I love you," I united
in His call.

How could it be any other way, for My Son is One
in Me, and I am One in Him and the Spirit?
This Trinity of love calls out to mankind from the
cross, and continues to call from the heart.

(*Romans 9:30*—He also called.)

8/1/98

Recall your love for Me every time you meet
someone, and treat him with love also.

(*Wisdom 19:16*—Welcoming them.)

8/1/98

A man is only truly a man, if he loves.

(*Sirach 30:22*—The very life of man.)

189.

8/2/98

Humor in life is important, for without it life would
become a misery.
It is important, however, that your humor does not
make life a misery for others by using their
weaknesses, their appearance, their state of
mind, their poverty, their family, their friends,
their mistakes, their mishaps, or their standing
in society as the means of your humor, for then
it is not fun at all...only sin.

(*Proverbs 15:28*—The just man weighs well his
utterance, but the mouth of the wicked pours
out evil.)

8/2/98

Care in your words, means consideration in your
heart.

(*Psalms 37:30-31*—Their tongues speak what is
right. God's teaching is in their hearts.)

8/2/98

Never say words intended to hurt; never say words
intended to demean; never say words filled with
hate, and then you will prevent many sins in
your life and in those who may respond to your
words in sin.

Words are very powerful, for they can spread love or
they can spread sin.
Be careful in what you say and how you say it.

(*2 Peter 1:5*—Make every effort.)

8/6/98

With joy in your heart, every moment is lived as it
    should be.
Everyone can find that joy in My Son Jesus, and
    find how life is meant to be.

(*1 Corinthians 15:22*—In Christ shall all be brought
    to life.)

8/6/98

Those who put money before God, run the risk of
    putting hell before heaven.

(*Wisdom 19:15*—What punishment was to be
    theirs.)

8/6/98

With peace in your heart, life becomes a joyful
    expression of My love.

(*Sirach 30:15*—Contentment of spirit.)
(*Luke 7:50*—Go in peace.)

8/6/98

To offer any suffering you endure to My Son Jesus
    on the Cross, brings you many graces for the
    good of others.
It is by your acceptance of your suffering for His
    glory that you show your love and are rewarded
    by Jesus from the Cross.

(*Lamentations 3:32*—In the abundance of His
    mercies.)

8/6/98

To relive your sins over and over, is unnecessary
and distracting.
Once you have confessed and been forgiven, do not
dwell on the past.
Remember not to make the same mistakes again,
but then let go of your past errors.

(*Lamentations 3:20*—Remembering it over and over
leaves my soul downcast within me.)

8/13/98

Treat each person with love,
Treat each person with respect,
Treat each person the way you would like to be
treated, for they like it, too.

8/13/98

Pray for the grace to do My will, and you will receive
it.

(*Isaiah 58:11*—Then the Lord will guide you always.)

8/13/98

A person who is aware of others' needs and
responds to them in love, is a person who
reflects My Son Jesus.

(*Matthew 25:46*—Blessed is that servant.)

8/13/98

Be at peace in the presence of Jesus.

(*Psalms 62:6*—Be at rest in God alone.)

8/13/98

Speak softly,
Speak kindly,
Speak lovingly,
For that is what My Son Jesus did, when He walked
the earth.

(*1 Corinthians 13:4*—Love is kind.)

8/17/98

Every morning, remember the gift of My love that is
before you in each day.

(*Psalms 123:2*—So our eyes are on the Lord, our
God.)

8/18/98

Sometimes people forget to love and then they
begin to suffer, for when love leaves, only pain
replaces it.

8/18/98

Be aware of how you can love others, and in doing
so, bring My love to them.
It is by service, humility, and caring.

(*Psalms 116:16*—Lord, I am your servant.)

193.

The certainty of My love is what sustained the
saints, and it must be this that sustains you.

(*Psalms 43:9*—Faithful love.)

8/20/98

In the past, many have given their lives for Me.
Today, many do also, and in the future many more
will.

Why do many people love Me so, that they would
sacrifice in this way for Me?

It is because they have discovered that loving Me
and having My love in their hearts, is worth
more than life itself...a discovery that all people
can make if only they look.

(*Psalms 57:11*—For your love towers to the
heavens.)

8/20/98

Love resides in every Eucharist.
Love exists in every Eucharist.
Love is every Eucharist.

(*Isaiah 30:20*—The Lord will give you the bread you
need.)

8/20/98

Love should be the foundation of a relationship
between a man and a woman, not physical
attraction.

(*Ephesians* 5:33—Each one of you should love his
wife as himself, and the wife should respect her
husband.)

8/25/98

As I watch each person live life, I look on in love,
waiting to give My love to each one.
As I watch each person live life, I smile with joy
each time they achieve goodness in their life.
As I watch each person live life, I give My help to
each one, hoping they will accept it and
recognize it.

Each one I love, and want to help bring goodness
into their life, so that one day they can come
home to Me, their Father, in heaven.

(*Psalms* 25:5—Guide me in Your truth and teach
me, for You are God my Savior.)

8/27/98

A man whose main reason for living is to love Me, is
a wise man.
A man whose main reason for living is to serve Me.
is a man who truly lives.
A man whose main reason for living is to share My
love in service of others, is a man who lives his
life wisely.

(*Daniel* 12:3—The wise.)

195.

8/27/98

Prayer can be done anywhere and any way, as long
as it is done in love.

(1 Corinthians 13:1—If I speak in human and
angelic tongues but do not have love, I am a
resounding gong or a clashing cymbal.)

8/28/98

As you look upon each day, look with wonder, look
with joy, and look with love...then you will begin
to appreciate what is given to you each time the
dawn breaks or evening sets.

(Jeremiah 23:24—Do I not fill both heaven and
earth?)

8/28/98

The joy of My love is to be found in each person, if
only you and they look.

(Isaiah 33:17—Your eyes will see.)

8/31/98

What joy, to love Me,
What peace, to know Me,
What hope, to believe in Me.

(Psalms 107:1—Give thanks to the Lord.)

9/1/98

As your Father, I love you,
As your Father, I hope for you.
As your Father, I offer help to you and to all people,
    for I love them and hope they will accept My
    help in their lives.

(*Zepheniah 2:10*—The people of the Lord.)

9/1/98

By the power of My Holy Spirit and the grace of My
    Son's love, all My children live, and they should
    forever thank God for that.

(*Psalms 33:9*—For He spoke, and it came to be.)

9/2/98

Take more care before you act on what others say.

(*2 Peter 2:3*—In their greed, they will exploit you
    with fabrications.)

9/2/98

A merciful heart forgives, loves, and welcomes all
    people.

This is My Son Jesus' heart.

(*1 Peter 1:3*—In His great mercy.)

197.

9/2/98

Spiritual gifts await,
Spiritual graces await,
Spiritual rewards await,
In the sacraments.

(Romans 16:2—That you may receive.)

9/2/98

A person who stands firm in the truth will live
    forever.

(Titus 1:9—Holding fast to the true message.)

9/2/98

In the divine heart of Jesus, is a place for each
    person, and in each person's human heart,
    should be a place for Jesus.

(Mark 12:30—You shall love the Lord, your God,
    with all your heart.)

9/6/98

The mystery of My love, is that it is eternal,
    universal, and never denied to anyone.
The mystery of My love, is that all things came to be
    and exist in My love.
The mystery of My love, is that every person has My
    love residing within his soul.
My mysterious love...which is Jesus.

(Colossians 1:15-16—He is the image of the invisible
    God, the first born of all creation, for in Him
    were created all things in heaven and on earth.)

9/12/98

Each person on earth is My child, and if you love
Me then you must love them, because they
come from Me.

(*Matthew 6:18*—Your Father.)

9/13/98

It is in the difficult moments you need to show love
and kindness more than ever.

(*Sirach 42:1*—Lest you sin.)

9/20/98

Never put your prayer aside because you are too
busy.
There is always time to pray and many ways to do
it; you only need to look and to make the effort.

(*Sirach 38:9*—Pray to God.)

9/20/98

It is when you show love through all difficulties,
that you show true love.

9/20/98

If you see every moment of your life as Mine, then it
is.

(*1 Corinthians 7:17*—Everyone should live as the
Lord has assigned.)

199.

9/20/98

In My love, all people are friends, all people are
family, and all people are loved.

(*Jeremiah 30:22*—My people.)

9/20/98

In each house, if My love resides there, you will feel
at home.

9/23/98

It is fear, that evil feeds on.
It is doubt, evil encourages.
It is uncertainty, evil tries to create.

(*Sirach 8:1*—Lest you fall into his power.)

9/23/98

It is through fear, evil causes many to sin.
It is in trust, that many overcome sin and find
security in Me.

(*Sirach 2:13*—Woe to the faint of heart, who trust
not.)

9/23/98

Generosity is in your heart; do not hide it.

(*Proverbs 22:9*—The kindly man will be blessed, for
he gives of his sustenance to the poor.)

9/24/98

With love in your heart, face each day and say,
"Lord I give this to you...every moment and
everything I do."
Then each day becomes another way to pray.

(*Acts 13:52*—Filled with joy and the Holy Spirit.)

9/27/98

A prayer to start the day,
A prayer throughout the day,
A prayer to end the day;
That is the way to pray.

(*Daniel 13:12*—Day by day.)

9/27/98

When your will is done, Mine is not.
When your needs come first, others do not.
When your life is the most important thing, service
is not.

Put yourself aside and follow My will in your life,
serving Me and serving the needs of others.
Make the most important thing in your life placing
God first, and then you will find eternal rewards
of love awaiting you in heaven.

(*John 12:26*—Whoever serves Me, must follow Me.)

9/28/98

Never discourage faith in any way; always support
it in love and with gentleness.

(*Psalms 141:4*—Do not let my heart incline to evil.)

201.

Love all you meet,
Love all you see,
Love all that exists,
For it all comes from Me.

(*Ecclesiasticus 5:19*—The joy of his heart.)

9/29/98

When you have love for all of creation, you have
love for Me.

(*Luke 1:47*—My spirit rejoices in God.)

10/1/98

As the angels gather around My throne singing My
praises, I look upon them and see their love for
Me and enjoy their worship of Me.
So it will be when mankind joins them, and unites
with the angels praising Me in eternity.
How I will enjoy this, and how I will enjoy the love
that will be shown.

(*Revelation 7:15*—For this reason, they stand
before God's throne and worship Him.)

10/1/98

Heaven's angels shine in My love.
Heaven's angels glow in My grace.
Heaven's angels exist in My glory.

(*Luke 1:26*—The angel.)

10/1/98

A day that heaven rejoices,
A day that heaven sings,
A day that heaven celebrates My wonderful servant,
St. Therese.

(*Malachi 3:22*—My servant.)

10/2/98

A gift of My love, sent to care for you and to be
there for you.
The gift of a guardian angel given to each person in
love.

(*Timothy 1:6*—The gift of God.)

10/3/98

Those who give will always receive.
Those who receive should always give.

(*Psalms 143:8*—Let Me hear of your kindness.)

10/10/98

To look at sin and to be attracted by it, will only
distract a person from looking to the truth and
living it.

(*Jeremiah 3:23*—Deceptive indeed.)

203.

<u>10/10/98</u>

A man who cannot live to the truth, is a man who
   courts disaster.

(*Ephesians 5:15*—Watch carefully, then, how you
   live.)
(*Matthew 6:1*—Take care.)
(*1 Corinthians 7:5*—So that Satan may not tempt
   you.)

<u>10/10/98</u>

To fear, is not to trust in Me.
To doubt, is not to believe in Me.
To worry, is not to give yourself to Me.
With trust in Me there is nothing to fear, and when
   you believe in Me, you never doubt that or
   worry about what may happen in your life.

(*Proverbs 3:5*—Trust in the Lord with all your
   heart.)

<u>10/10/98</u>

To be free, you must live in Me; anything else is
   slavery.

(*Romans 8:15*—For you did not receive a spirit of
   slavery.)

<u>10/11/98</u>

The precious gift of life must never be denied, for to
   do so for any reason, is to offend Me, your God,
   and to condemn yourself to a punishment you
   would not want to receive.

(*Isaiah 17:11*—On the day of the grievous blow.)

10/11/98

With love in your eyes you see love everywhere,
  even in the hearts of those who hide it in sin.

(*John 18:8*—If you are looking for Me.)

10/24/98

The miracle of life today is often seen only as a
  process of nature, and the gift I give is often
  ignored.
The first heartbeat, the first breath, do not just
  happen as a physical action, for something is
  needed for them to occur.
That something is the fire of life I put into each
  being, and allow to be expressed in a physical
  way on earth.
This fire should be encouraged to burn brightly to
  warm creation in a special way, not
  extinguished, leaving a coldness in the void
  where it should have been.

Life is a precious gift of love, which today is
  attacked by the evils of self, of pride, and of
  hatred.

No wonder the world suffers so much today, and
  unless mankind begins to appreciate, treasure,
  and celebrate life for what it is, then tomorrow
  it will suffer even more.

(*Wisdom 12:15*—You regard it as unworthy.)
(*Proverbs 9:12*—And if you are arrogant, you alone
  shall bear it.)

205.

10/24/98

Kindness shows love,
Selfishness shows sin.

(*Psalms 103:8*—Abounding in kindness.)

10/24/98

Never look down upon another, for in My eyes all
    are equal.

(*Romans 12:16*—Do not be haughty.)
(*James 4:6*—God resists the proud, but gives graces
    to the humble.)

10/24/98

Each breath, is a gift I give to you.
Each heartbeat, is a sign of My love for you.
Each moment you live, is the gift of life I give to
    you.
When you do My will with each one of them, you
    return My love to Me, wrapped in yours.

(*Psalms 68:19*—Live in the presence of God.)

10/24/98

Your love is what I ask.
My love is what I offer, and when your love is given
    to Me in an acceptance of My love, this union
    will bring you to true life.

(*Romans 8:28*—For those who love God.)
(*Proverbs 2:19*—Gain the paths of life.)

10/26/98

One, Holy, Catholic, and Apostolic Church is the
Church My Son Jesus founded, and it is the
Church all who love God should belong to, for it
is the Church of God.

(*Isaiah 56:6*—Who join themselves to the Lord
ministering to Him.)

10/26/98

In prayer, feel My love,
In prayer, feel My presence,
In prayer, feel My grace filling you.

(*Matthew 6:5*—When you pray.)

10/29/98

With love in the center of your heart, your heart
becomes one in Jesus, for He is love and His
love is found in the Eucharist, so fill your heart
there.

(*John 5:42*—The love of God.)

10/29/98

There is a constant battle in the world of good
   against evil.
This battle is part of everyone's life, and when each
   person makes the decision to accept My Son
   Jesus' victory on the cross, the battle in his
   life is won.

With each defeat of evil, the world as a whole
   changes, and goodness grows in strength, until
   one day all evil will leave the earth.
It is important all persons know this, and make
   the effort to break the chains of sin in their
   lives, for when they do so, they become part of
   the army of love that is guaranteed success,
   through My Son's sacrifice on the cross.

(*Psalms 1:5*—The wicked will not survive.)

10/29/98

If you speak of love,
If you try to live in love,
If you seek only love, you have nothing to fear, for
   Jesus will be with you in His divine love.

(*Thessalonians 1:4*—Loved by God.)

10/29/98

Life is only a moment in eternity.
Live it wisely, or you risk losing it in eternal
   darkness.

(*Wisdom 5:15*—The just live forever.)

10/30/98

I call upon the weak and make them strong in Me,
  but, continuously, I remind them of their
  weaknesses, so that they know it is only in Me
  all comes to be.

(*Sirach 1:1*—All wisdom comes from the Lord, and
  with Him it remains forever.)

10/30/98

Love must be in your heart always, for the moment
  it isn't, you allow evil a chance to enter.

(*Job 9:4*—Wise in heart.)

11/1/98

The saints show how, with trust in Me and with
  perseverance through difficult moments, lives
  can become miraculous reflections of My love.

(*Jeremiah 31:21*—Set up road markers, put up
  guideposts.)

11/2/98

Each holy soul you pray for, will remember you in
  heaven, and will pray for you to join them there.

(*Psalms 32:5*—Thus should all you faithful pray.)

209.

11/2/98

From within your heart, if you reach out in love to
Me, you will find I will respond in ways beyond
your understanding, but ways that only bring
you happiness and love.

(*John 17:22*—And your hearts will rejoice.)

11/2/98

To make this day Mine, love all you meet, and do it
in a way that brings My love to them.

(*Psalms 128:3*—Like a fruitful vine.)

6/11/98

When prayer is hard, know in these moments I am
with you and I am helping you, and that by
these moments I am strengthening your heart.

(*Jeremiah 51:29*—The Lord's plan.)

11/6/98

The love you have in your heart will grow in service
of Me and service of others.

(*Ecclesiasticus 11:5*—The work of God.)

11/6/98

It is true wisdom to try and live to My
commandments; it is folly not to.

(*Ecclesiasticus 4:17*—Let your approach be
obedience rather than the fool's offering of
sacrifice, for they know not how to keep from
doing evil.)

11/9/98

A man must repay his debts, otherwise he is taking
advantage of others.

(*Job 31:28*—This, too, would be a crime for
condemnation.)

11/17/98

As the day begins, offer it to Me in love.
As the day passes, offer it to Me in love.
As the day ends, offer it to Me in love.

Then you make your day truly Mine.

(*Psalms 91:16*—Length of days.)

11/17/98

In every heart is the need to be loved, and that need
can only truly be fulfilled in My Son Jesus.

(*Luke 16:15*—God knows your hearts.)

211.

I look upon the world and see all the love that is
  wasted, and all the sin that is accepted.
I look with sadness at how easily goodness is
  rejected and evil embraced.
I look in the hope that many will change and accept
  the love I offer, and stop wasting the wonderful
  gift of life I have given to them.

(*Psalms 100:3*—Our Maker, to whom we belong.)

11/20/98

Time has no power over Jesus My Son, for it is in
  Him and through Him time came to be.
From the beginning He was with Me, and forever He
  is with Me, united in My spirit and in My love;
  Master of all ages.
Time, a servant to God; not God a servant to time.

(*Job 8:7*—Time.)
(*Psalms 24:1*—Is the Lords' and all it holds.)
(*Sirach 39:20*—His gaze spans all the ages.)

11/20/98

Each day is a miracle—never forget that.

(*Sirach 7:36*—In whatever you do, remember your
  last days.)

11/20/98

To trust is not foolish, but it is wise to be careful in
  whom you trust.

(*Philippians 2:22*—Know his worth.)

11/20/98

In My son Jesus, time is divided, and yet it is one.

(*Sirach 1:1*—And with Him, it remains forever.)

11/22/98

The reign of peace will come to earth when all of
mankind accepts Jesus as their king.

(*Acts 15:17*—Even all the Gentiles.)

11/23/98

The fire of My love can touch many hearts by the
power of prayer, so never stop praying for this
to happen.

(*Matthew 6:6*—Pray to your Father.)

11/26/98

The Trinity of love is beyond the understanding of
man, for his reason, science, and intelligence
are incapable of coming to terms with the
absolute truth of God.

(*Mark 7:18*—Without understanding.)

213.

11/26/98

The power of My love, is seen in Jesus.
The strength of My love, is seen in Jesus.
The mercy of My love. is seen in Jesus.

Jesus is My love, and Jesus showed the power My
love has over evil...as with the strength of My
love, He showered My mercy upon the world.

(*Ephesians 6:22*—I am sending Him to you for this
very purpose.)

11/26/98

With a prayer in your heart, your heart is open to
Me.

(*Sirach 39:35*—With full joy of heart.)

11/27/98

To imitate Jesus in your life, means to carry your
cross without complaining.

(*Jeremiah 6:7*—Ever before me are wounds and
blows.)

11/29/98

A precious gift is in each person, and when you can
see this in all those you meet, is when you can
begin to truly love them.

(*1 Timothy 4:4*—Everything created by God is good.)

11/29/98

Never dismiss the concerns of another as
    unimportant, for to them it could be very
    important, and it could be a way they
    strengthen or weaken their faith.

(*2 Corinthians 4:16*—Therefore we are not
    discouraged.)

12/1/98

Surrounded with the love of Jesus, you and
    everyone else who embrace His love are safe
    and protected from all evil.

(*Psalms 138:7*—Your right hand saves me.)

12/1/98

If money clouds your sight, soon love will go.

(*Psalms 73:7*—Out of their stupidity comes sin.)

12/1/98

Love must be given freely to all people.
Love must not be only for those to whom you are
    close.
Love must be there to share with all people, for if
    you keep love to yourself and those close to you,
    it is not true love at all, only selfishness.

(*Haggai 2:19*—Indeed, the seed has not sprouted.)

215.

12/1/98

Those who profess to love God, must bring others to
love Me; otherwise their love is a self-centered
love, and not the love I want My children to
have.

(*Psalms 103:2*—Do not forget.)

12/9/98

If all of My children embrace My love, all of them
will be happy.

(*Proverbs 8:32*—O children, listen to Me.)

12/9/98

I created animals in My love, and if you love Me,
you should love My creations and treat them
with respect.

(*Psalms 33:4*—All His works.)

12/9/98

Make your ways My ways, and find your life will be
fruitful.

(*Ezekiel 17:23*—And bear fruit.)

12/10/98

Sanctity comes through complete obedience to My will.
Holiness comes from a complete love of Me.
Sainthood comes when a person lives in My love trying to do My will, accepting this as the complete truth in life.

(*Sirach 46:6*—Because he was a devoted follower of God.)

12/10/98

When someone is sick, they need help.
Whether it is sickness of mind, of body, or of soul, none should be turned away and all should be helped, for this is part of loving Me.

(*Romans 8:9*—Whoever does not have the Spirit of Christ, does not belong to Him.)

12/10/98

Be patient with those who frustrate you, because they may have a problem within and need help, not condemnation.

(*Matthew 5:44*—Pray for those who persecute you.)

12/10/98

Misery within comes from sin in your life, for this is what sin brings...not happiness, only pain and suffering.

(*Lamentations 3:39*—In the face of his sins.)
(*Psalms 51:19*—Is a broken spirit.)

217.

12/11/98

Today, like every day is a gift; appreciate it and
    enjoy it, as you should with all My gifts.

(*Malachi 3:23*—The day of the Lord.)

12/11/98

An immigrant should not ignore or try to forget his
    heritage or the people and country he comes
    from, for in every culture is a richness to be
    learned.
When this is ignored or forgotten, then often so
    much is lost, and people run the risk of
    throwing away what generations have passed on
    to them, and what I, in My love, may have given
    to mankind to help them live a better life.

(*Job 8:13*—Everyone who forgets God.)

12/12/98

Gentleness always overcomes,
Softness always wins,
Love always is victorious,
And this is what My Son Jesus showed in His life.

(*Luke 1:25*—So has the Lord done.)

12/13/98

If you hurt people, even unintentionally, you
    must do all you can to help them overcome their
    pain, and you must try to help them see you
    meant no harm.

(*Psalms 81:7*—I relieved their shoulders of the
    burden.)

12/15/98

Kindness breeds love,
Anger breeds hatred.

(*Titus 3:2*—To be peaceable, considerate, exercising all graciousness toward everyone.)

12/15/98

If only My children on earth accepted Me as their Father and lived in the way I asked, happiness would be the way of the world, not suffering.

(*Isaiah 58:2*—And not abandoned the law of their God.)

12/16/98

Innocent hearts,
Innocent minds,
Innocent souls,
Are found in the young, and with prayers, guidance, and help, they can stay that way.

(*1 Corinthians 9:11*—If we have sown spiritual seeds.)
(*Wisdom 9:4*—Among your children.)

12/16/98

The future always looks bright, if you love Me.

(*John 14:15*—If you love Me.)

219.

12/16/98

Your heart should always be open, offering love to
all you meet, for when you do this, then you
start to imitate My Son Jesus, Whose heart has
never been and never will be closed to any.

(*1 Corinthians 9:14*—In the same way.)

12/16/98

There are many in need, and yet there are many
who have more than they need.
There are many who suffer, and yet there are many
who are able to prevent or reduce the suffering
in the world.
There are many who hunger, and yet there are
many who waste what would feed the poor.

Until those who can prevent suffering, can feed the
hungry, and can fill the needs of the poor,
accept their responsibilities and do so, sin will
not leave the earth.

(*Nahum 1:7*—Take care of those.)

12/16/98

Each Mass you celebrate, is a step closer to Me.
Each Eucharist you receive, is leading you closer to
Me.
Each time you receive the Eucharist in the
celebration of the Mass, you are led a step
closer to Me by My Son Jesus, Who is the
Eucharist.

(*Matthew 27:59*—Taking the body.)
(*2 Peter 1:1*—Of our God and Savior, Jesus Christ.)

12/17/98

A new day dawns and brings a new opportunity to
show your love for Me, and a new opportunity to
bring My love to others.

(*John 1:31*—That He might be made known.)

12/17/98

There is a longing within each person to be loved
and to love.
There is a longing within each person to be cared
for and to have someone to care for.
There is a longing within each person that can only
be truly satisfied if they know and love Me;
otherwise, this longing may be turned to one of
self, and may be hidden under the layers of sin
that come with selfishness.

(*Psalms 117:8*—Better to take refuge in the Lord.)

12/17/98

Many disasters happen around the world, and each
one is an opportunity for people to show they
love and care for each other.

(*Ephesians 5:16*—Making the most of every
opportunity.)

12/21/98

Throughout history I have called people from all
walks of life to spread My word, and throughout
history, many have denied this would be so.

(*Isaiah 9:10*—The Lord raises up.)

221.

To live by the truth is difficult for many today.
It seems to be far easier to live by the deceit of sin
    instead.
No wonder the world suffers, and no wonder so
    many despair.
The rewards of evil are obvious, for they can be
    seen everywhere on the earth.
Yet mankind continues to be deceived, and walks
    the path of self-destruction.

Now is the time eyes were opened to see what is the
    truth, and the truth is that unless mankind
    returns to Me through My Son Jesus, it will
    bring upon itself more suffering and pain, and
    many will deny themselves eternal life with Me
    in heaven.

(Isaiah 17:10—You have forgotten God, your
    Savior.)
(Proverbs 13:15—The way of the faithless is their
    ruin.)

12/21/98

Go in love to the Eucharist, and then be filled with
    love in Jesus in the Eucharist.

(Luke 11:3—Give us each day our daily bread.)

12/23/98

If you harbor angry thoughts of another, they can
soon lead you into sin, if you are not careful.
If you harbor angry thoughts, how can you expect
to serve Me?
If you harbor angry thoughts, do you think it will be
possible to imitate My Son Jesus?

(*Ecclesiasticus 10:20*—In your thoughts.)
(*Sirach 16:18*—My ways.)

12/23/98

It is when you let your peace be disturbed, you give
evil a way in.

(*Isaiah 26:3*—Keep in peace.)

12/27/98

One day a man came across a dead bird on the side
of the road.
He looked down at the bird, feeling sad that such a
beautiful creature had to die.
He studied the colors of the bird and was deeply
touched by their depth and natural beauty.
"How sad," he thought, "that this bird would not
be able to bring its majesty to the world
anymore."

Just then, the man heard another bird singing in
the trees and looked up to see a similar bird
sitting on a branch above him.
The colors of this one were almost the same as the
dead one, but because of the life in this bird,
the colors seemed more vibrant.

223.

The man smiled as he thought, "Well, God gives us
many gifts of beauty, and now this dead bird's
time has come, but here in this other bird, the
gift of God's love continues."

He bent down and dug a little hole and placed the
dead bird in it saying, "Thank you, Lord, for
this gift, and for all the gifts You give to us."
As he was saying this, the bird in the tree was
singing joyfully.

The man thought to himself, "That bird is enjoying
life, and I am sure this dead bird did the same
when he lived.
These birds seem to live each moment as a joy with
little concern for the future.
They live bringing God's gift in them wherever they
go.

Maybe that's how I should be, not so concerned for
the future, but living each moment for the gift it
is, and trying to bring that gift of God's love in
my life, wherever I go."

He walked on noticing each bird in the trees around
him, and soaking in the beautiful songs they
sang.

"From now on," he thought to himself, "I will sing a
beautiful song from my soul to God, wherever I
go, and maybe by the grace of God, I will bring
joy to others, just as these birds are bringing
joy to me."

With a smile on his face he continued his walk, a
walk that would bring him closer to God, and a
walk that would make his life, and the lives of
those he met, more joyful.

(*Deuteronomy 32:3*—For I will sing the Lord's
renown. Oh, proclaim the greatness of our God.)

12/27/98

The Holy Family showed that families are My gift,
and that family life lived in love will bring that
family to sanctification.

(*Colossians 3:20*—For this is pleasing to the Lord.)

12/27/98

In a family are the foundations of society, for when
families live in love and share that love with
others, then society itself becomes one of love.

(*1 Peter 3:8*—Be of one mind, sympathetic, loving
toward one another, compassionate.)

12/31/98

Fear, traps your soul,
Trust in Me, sets it free.

(*Matthew 27:43*—He trusted in God.)

12/31/98

To break free from the yoke of sin is the call to the
followers of Jesus, not to embrace it.

(*Mark 9:42*—A great millstone.)

<u>12/31/98</u>

When you come to understand that I am the Truth,
and you believe in and place yourself in the
Truth, you should never fear evil, for the Truth
always wins.

(*Acts 18:9-10*—Do not be afraid; go on speaking and
do not be silent, for I am with you.)

<u>1/2/99</u>

The Church must be Eucharistic.
The people must live a Eucharistic life.
The world will then change, and all because of the
Eucharist.

(*Psalms 95:7*—For this is our God.)

<u>1/4/99</u>

Pray often,
Pray with love,
Pray in hope,
And believe that I will answer your prayers for good,
because I will.

(*Baruch 4:21*—Call upon God.)
(*Philippians 1:4*—Praying always.)

<u>1/5/99</u>

A hardened heart is easily led into sin, and then it
becomes a suffering heart that brings pain to
itself and many others.

(*Luke 24:38*—Your hearts.)
(*Jeremiah 17:4*—Will enslave you.)

<u>1/5/99</u>

With care and love, all people can become the true
children of God they were created to be.

(*Ephesians 1:14*—Our inheritance.)

<u>1/5/99</u>

Remember, you pray in all you do when you offer it
to Me.

<u>1/5/99</u>

Wisdom does not come with age, but it comes with
love.

(*Jeremiah 22:16*—True knowledge.)
(*Job 34:2*—Hear, O wise men.)

<u>1/6/99</u>

Many times I offer people the chance to do My work,
but so often those who do accept, end up doing
what they want.

Always seek to do My will by prayer, the
sacraments, Holy Scripture, and obedience to
the Church.
If you do this, it is less likely you will do your will,
and more certain you will do Mine.

(*Deuteronomy 5:32*—Be careful, therefore, to do as
the Lord, your God, has commanded you, not
turning aside to the right or to the left.)
(*Deuteronomy 5:33*—But following exactly the way
prescribed to you by the Lord, your God.)

227.

1/6/99

It is impossible to know true love without knowing
  Me, for I am love.

(*Acts 4:20*—It is impossible.)

1/6/99

If you live a life without love in it, then you will live
  far away from Me.

As I am love, love must reside in your heart, must
  fill your life, and must be your reason for living;
  otherwise, you cannot claim to be truly Mine.

(*1 Corinthians 2:9*—Those who love Him.)

1/7/99

If a man does not work, he loses part of his dignity.
If a man does not work, at times he feels unworthy.
If a man does not work, often he becomes a burden
  on others.

A man must work for the good of himself and the
  good of others.

(*Proverbs 26:16*—Good sense.)

1/7/99

The Church must stand firm in My truth and love,
  no matter how the world assails it.
Mankind's changing opinions and laws cannot alter
  My truth.
Mankind's sins cannot change My love, and so it
  must be with My Church; it must not change to
  suit mankind.

The Church must be a bastion of hope in a world
filled with despair.
The Church must stand high above the turmoil in
the world.
The Church must be obedient to My will, and by its
obedience bring all of mankind to be the same.

The Church must be for all peoples and deny none.
The Church must open its arms in love, even to its
fiercest opponent.

The Church must bring the graces and gifts I give
to it, to every corner of the earth.
The Church must be universal in its love of Me, and
keep to the guidelines that Jesus My Son gave
to it.
The Church must remain true to the Catholic name
it bears, for the Church is My light in the world,
and to shine brightly, it must be as I ask.

(1 Thessalonians 4:2—For you know what
instructions we gave you through the Lord
Jesus.)
(2 John:3—In truth and love.)

1/8/99

Never alter the truth even a little, for then it is no
longer the truth but a deception.

(John 18:37—Testify to the truth.)

1/8/99

To try and overcome sin by using sin to do so, only
multiplies evil and helps sin to grow.

(Luke 6:35—Do good.)
(Isaiah 48:2—Rely on the God of Israel.)

229.

Love forgives,
Love understands,
Love offers help to those in need and forgives their
   mistakes, understanding what caused them to
   sin, and offers them help not to sin again.

(*Philemon 9*—Out of love.)

1/8/99

If someone does not listen to good advice, that is
   their choice; you cannot force them.
Advise them, pray for them, and then let them
   decide, for it is their right to choose.

(*Job 5:8*—I would appeal to God.)

1/9/99

Anger does not change hearts for the better, only
   for the worse.

(*Jeremiah 6:24*—Anguish takes hold.)

1/9/99

At the time of My Son's death, My divine love flowed
   through His wounds...One in His divine love,
   showering forgiveness on the world.

(*Hebrews 9:20*—This is the blood of the covenant
   which God has enjoined upon you.)

1/11/99

In the times you feel I am far away from you, know I
am as close as ever.

(*1 Corinthians 8:8*—Closer to God.)

1/11/99

The light has come into the world, but many have
remained in darkness.
The light has come into the world and darkness
tries to hide it.
The light has come into the world and darkness
cannot remain, no matter how hard darkness
tries to hide this truth.

(*John 8:12*—Jesus spoke to them again saying, "I
am the light of the world."

1/11/99

Saints are the proof that all of mankind, if it tries
to live as I ask, can spend eternity in My love.

(*Joel 2:11*—Does His bidding.)

1/12/99

Take your time in all you do, for if you hurry, you
may make mistakes in your eagerness to be
finished.

(*Proverbs 18:2*—He who acts hastily, blunders.)

231.

Look at the palm of your hand and see the gift I
   give to you, and know that mankind with all its
   science and technology cannot create one thing
   to compare with this.

(2 Corinthians 5:1—Made with hands, eternal in
heaven.)

1/12/99

If you look upon a flower and see My love, you look
   with eyes open to the truth.
If you look and see nothing, then you truly are
   blind.

(Acts 26:18—Open their eyes, that they may turn
   from darkness to light.)

1/12/99

All are called to a vocation in their lives.
For some, it is within the Church, for others it is
   within the family or within society, but for all
   there is a place and a way to serve Me in life on
   earth.

(Deuteronomy 5:33—The way prescribed for you by
   the Lord your God.)

1/12/99

Prayer is a gift that is often under-estimated, but
   never over-estimated.

(Colossians 4:2—Persevere in prayer.)

1/16/99

Each day is a gift I give to you...a gift which you
    can return to Me wrapped in your love, if you
    try.

(*Matthew 5:23*—Bring your gift to the altar.)

1/16/99

Love was showered on the world from the Cross,
    and the world only needs to stand under this
    shower of love to be saved.
Each drop of Blood was a drop of love, waiting to fill
    hearts and souls.
Each drop of Blood was a river of forgiveness,
    waiting to flood the lives of mankind with divine
    mercy.
Each drop of Blood was a call to all people from My
    Son Jesus, to say, "I love you."

(*Philippians 2:17*—Poured out as a libation.)

1/18/99

To see love everywhere,
To feel joy in everything,
To care for everyone,

This is what many of the saints did, and people
    today need to do the same, if many of them
    want to be saints also.

(*1 Peter 2:21*—For to this you have been called.)

233.

1/18/99

Always love, no matter what the situation, for if
you do not love, you step away from Me.

(1 Timothy 2:15—Persevere in faith, and love, and
holiness.)

1/18/99

The more you speak of My love, the more My word
will touch the hearts of those who listen.

(Deuteronomy 6:6—Take to heart these words.)

1/18/99

In Holy Scripture, you will find all you need to live.
In Holy Scripture, you will find all you need to
grow.
In Holy Scripture, you will find all you need to come
to heaven, for in Holy Scripture, I give you,
through My Son Jesus, the way to find heaven.

(Psalms 103:7—His ways were revealed.)

1/18/99

Come to Me in love, and find your love grow.

(1 Thessalonians 4:10—To progress even more.)

1/20/99

Obedience is the only way you must walk.
Without obedience, you will stumble and fall.

(Sirach 3:6—He obeys the Lord.)

1/20/99

In some hearts there are barriers, while in others
there are none.

This is part of the freedom that mankind has, and it
is a wonderful gift that I give so that all can
choose freely to love Me.

(*1 John 3:1*—See what love the Father has bestowed
on us, that we may be called the children of
God.)

1/20/99

To walk in obedience to Me, means to walk towards
holiness.

(*2 Chronicles 35:26*—In the law of the Lord.)

1/22/99

In sickness and in health, a person should never
stop loving Me.
In good times and in difficult times, a person
should never stop loving Me.
In wealth and in poverty, a person should never
stop loving Me.

If they do, the person risks losing the greatest
treasure of all, My love.

(*Psalms 31:24*—Love the Lord, all you faithful.)

1/22/99

The pressure of work for many today, brings
    distress into their lives.
The financial burdens placed upon many today,
    brings despair into their lives.
The right to have food to eat, a roof over your head,
    and security in life, should not bring so many
    financial burdens into people's lives, that they
    are pressured into working more than they can
    cope with.

It is the right of each person to live well without
    having to pay a heavy price for it;
A right that many in power try to take away from
    those less fortunate; and, to take away
    someone's God-given right, is a sin that will
    have to be answered for.

(*Wisdom 4:17*—Do not understand what the Lord
    intended.)

1/22/99

To argue stubbornly with people over decisions they
    have made, will often only harden their heart.
Responding humbly in love and with patience,
    causing no offence to the other, is the way to
    change hearts and to guide them into the right
    decisions.

(*Sirach 7:17*—Humble your pride.)

1/24/99

Even to accept one little sin in your life, is to allow
    evil to take a foothold, and to give evil the
    opportunity to lead you into eternal suffering.

(*Hosea 1:2*—Turning away from the Lord.)

1/26/99

Love is not selective,
Love is not restrictive,
Love is not destructive.

When you truly love, your heart is open to all,
    restricting no one from your love.
When you truly love, there is no selection of who
    you will love, for you love all.
When you truly love, you do not destroy other
    people's lives, but you build them up and
    encourage them, for you realize they are as
    important as you.

(*John 15:17*—This I command you: love one
    another.)
(*2 Corinthians 10:8*—Building you up.)

1/26/99

A person's heart was created from My love to bring
    love wherever it goes.
A person's heart was created from My love to grow
    in love throughout its life on earth.
A person's heart was created from My love to
    return to My love, once its time on earth is
    complete.

It is by bringing My love wherever one goes, that a
    person's heart will lovingly grow.
Then, in eternity, a person can come home to Me to
    share in the joy that is heavenly.

(*Isaiah 56:7*—Joyful in My house.)

237.

1/30/99

To long for the Eucharist is a grace that will grow, if
you allow it, by thinking on what Jesus gives to
you in each One...He gives you Himself.

(*1 Timothy 4:4*—When received with thanksgiving.)

1/31/99

The church is alive in the sacraments.
The people cannot truly live without them.

When the people of the Church live the sacramental
life, then the living Church will change the
world.

(*Psalms 103:2*—Do not forget all the gifts of God.)

2/2/99

Prayer is to strengthen,
Prayer is to grow,
Prayer is to love.

When you pray from your heart, you grow in My
love and find the strength you need to do My
will.

(*1 Timothy 4:5*—Made holy by the invocation of God
in prayer.)

2/2/99

The way of Jesus My Son, is the way all people
should follow, for it is My way, and there is no
other way that leads to heaven.

(*Wisdom 19:17*—The entrance.)

2/4/99

The love I have for mankind can be found in Holy
Scripture.

It is clearly and plainly shown there, in the life of
My Son Jesus.

Mankind, if it looks with an open heart, will see
how much I love it, and how I long for mankind
to love Me.

(*Matthew 20:34*—They received their sight and
followed Him.)

2/4/99

The joy you feel when you see someone you love
filled with happiness, is a gift of My love, which
you should help grow by feeling this way
whenever you see anyone happy, for you should
love them all.

(*Isaiah 66:14*—When you see this, your heart shall
rejoice.)
(*Psalms 90:14*—Sing for joy.)

2/5/99

In every country,
In every town,
In every life,
I am there, for I am everywhere.

239.

2/5/99

To look at a person and only to see his outer
    beauty, is a blindness of heart.
When you look upon another, look within and see
    his true beauty, not just that which is on the
    surface.

(*Matthew 7:5*—Then you will see clearly.)

2/5/99

Each time you think of the saints with love in your
    heart, they bring that love, joined with theirs,
    as a gift to Me.

2/10/99

There are many beliefs in the world, but only one is
    true, and that is Jesus is My only Son, and with
    the Holy Spirit, is One in Me.

Any other belief comes from darkness, and is there
    to destroy souls.

(*Baruch 6:72*—It can be known that they are not
    God's.)

2/10/99

A brave heart is one that loves Me through all
    adversity.

(*Sirach 22:23*—In time of trouble, remain true to
    Him.)

2/10/99

An honest heart will always be secure.

(*Zechariah 5:10*—With Me.)

2/12/99

By the Body and Blood of Jesus, mankind is united to Me.
It is only by its free choice, mankind can break this bond.

(*John 19:1*—Given to you from above.)

2/12/99

The gift of life I give to you must be treasured and nutured in My love, to grow and to become what it was meant to be, a celebration of My love.

(*Proverbs 29:13*—The Lord gives.)
(*Matthew 10:39*—Life.)

2/12/99

Do not try to imitate anyone except My Son Jesus and those who have imitated Him in their lives.

(*Luke 1:75*—In holiness and righteousness.)

2/14/99

Trust is a sign of love, for without trust, how can you truly love?

241.

Each person must be shown the same love; none
must be preferred over others.

When you can do this, then you imitate My love, for
I love all mankind the same.

(*Philippians 3:17*—Imitators of Me.)

2/15/99

A prayerful man,
A scriptural man,
A sacramental man...
Is a man of God, when he is also a loving man.

(*1 Timothy 2:15*—In faith and love and holiness.)

6/16/99

The future looks bright, when you think of My light.

The future looks dim, when you think of self and
sin.

(*Isaiah 58:10*—Light shall rise for you in the
darkness.)

2/17/99

The truth never hurts, unless you live in sin.

2/17/99

Many people today are confused sexually into believing sex is only an act that has little meaning, other than one's enjoyment.

Sex should be an expression of a married couples' love, and is made holy by the Sacrament of Marriage.
Sex is the gift I give, so that mankind can take part in My creative love.
Sex, when it is not kept and seen for the gift of love it is meant to be, becomes another way that Satan can trap unsuspecting humans into giving him their very souls.

(*2 Maccabees 6:1*—And live no longer by the laws of God.)

2/20/99

A spiritual grace is granted each time you pray, so never stop praying.

2/24/99

The crosses each person carries are graces of love offered through My Son Jesus.
It is when you accept these crosses and offer them to Jesus in love, that you grow in grace.

2/25/99

Peace in your life can only come in a true way with Jesus My Son in your heart.

(*Job 11:19*—And you shall take your rest with none to disturb.)

243.

2/25/99

Within humanity are many weaknesses, but within
My love, they can all be overcome.

(*Ezekiel 17:24*—And make the withered tree bloom.)

2/25/99

In nature, if you look, you will see My love
everywhere.
You only need to look in love.

(*Jeremiah 11:17*—The Lord of Hosts Who planted
you.)

2/25/99

It is wise to hold your tongue, rather than say an
unkind word about another.

2/27/99

Be at peace, knowing I love you.

2/27/99

It is by love you must live...My love.
It is by trust you must live...trust in Me.
It is by hope you must live...hope that I will give
you all you need in your life, when you trust in
My love for you.

2/28/99

Persevere in loving, for it is truly the only way to
heaven.

(*Psalms 71:6*—My hope in You never waivers.)
(*Job 6:1*—That I should endure.)

2/28/99

Only be concerned with doing My will, and then
everything else will be given to you.

(*Romans 7:25*—Serve the law of God.)

3/1/99

All prayer is heard by Me and answered in the way
that is best.
Even when you think your prayers are weak, know
that I listen.

3/1/99

Each step towards Me is a step to eternal bliss, and
each step must be one of love; otherwise it is a
step away from Me.

3/4/99

When your stomach is full and you feel content,
think of those with empty stomachs and only
feelings of despair in their lives.

Think of how you can help them.

(And, the messages continue...)

ΑΩ